CW00448839

Gameful Writing

Seven People, Seven Stories, Seven Lessons Learned

Victoria Ichizli-Bartels

Gameful Writing
Seven People, Seven Stories, Seven Lessons Learned

Book 4 in Series "Gameful Life"

1st Edition

Copyright © 2020 Victoria Ichizli-Bartels

The moral right of the author has been asserted.

All rights reserved.

This is a work of fiction. Names, characters, places, and incidents are the product of the author's imagination or are used fictitiously. Any resemblance to actual events, organizations, or persons, living or dead, is coincidental.

All trademarks and brands mentioned in this book are used fictitiously because they fit organically into the story and made it sound more realistic. All of the trademarks and brands are used to the benefit of the trademark owner, with no intention of infringement of the trademark. Where such designations appear in this book, and where the author (and publisher) was aware of that claim, and rather than putting a trademark symbol after every occurrence of a trademarked name, they have been capitalized. The trademarks and brands are proprietary to their owners and are not affiliated with this document in any way.

This book is fictional, but it contains some how-to recommendations like in a self-help book. The content provided hereof is based on the author's opinion and personal experiences and observations. Every effort has been made to ensure that the content provided in this book is accurate and helpful. However, the author of this book does not dispense any medical or legal advice. The intent of the author is only to offer information of a general nature to help you in your quest for well-being. In the event you use any of the information in this book for yourself, which is your constitutional right, the author (who is also the publisher) assumes no responsibility for your actions.

The author reserves the right to make any changes she deems necessary to future versions of the publication to ensure its accuracy.

No part of this publication may be reproduced, stored in or introduced into a retrieval system or transmitted, in any form or by any means (electronic, mechanical, photocopying, recording or otherwise), without the prior written permission of the author.

Cover design by Alice Jago

Optimist Writer

For LeAnne,

Thank you for giving me the chance to teach writing.

and

For the Black Label Writers' Club in Aalborg,

Thank you for being such a fantastically inspiring and supportive group.

"I learned that when you play golf you're actually supposed to play golf. It's a game. You play it. You don't think it.

"It's before and after a round that you do your thinking, your analysis, your practicing.

...

"When you write, you should write. You should play. Then you balance that with analysis and learning and training and drills."

— James Scott Bell, *The Mental Game of Writing*

Table of Contents

Chapter 1: Miriam

*

Miriam couldn't believe what she had just done.

She had agreed to help one of the people she detested most.

Will had had the nerve to contact her on almost the anniversary of her best friend's death.

His girlfriend's death. Miriam bet he hadn't remembered the date. It didn't matter that it was five years since Lily had died and that Will was a man. Even a regular man should be capable of remembering such things. But not Will. He wasn't regular. He was one of the worst.

If it really hurt as much as he'd claimed, in his drunken state after the funeral, then he should remember. But Miriam was sure he didn't. He'd been drunk for most of Lily's illness; when she was bed-ridden and needed extra care both at home and in hospital. Which lasted almost six months. Six! No wonder Will became an alcoholic. Miriam had helped Will's mother get a key to his apartment, to collect some belongings for his stay in rehab.

What could Will know about loss? Nothing!

But Miriam knew loss. She knew it too well. Both her parents had died in short succession when she was just a teenager. Her mother in a car accident, and her father from a heart attack. And just a couple of years after Miriam and Lily met, Lily had died too.

Miriam didn't know why she'd remained in Aalborg the five years since. It was more time than she had known Lily. Maybe it was her job that kept her here. Maybe. Thankfully it was going well.

Miriam had been unable to form a new friendship or relationship since Lily's death.

She was afraid that if she let anyone get as close as she'd been to her parents and to Lily, that she would lose them too. To grieve for three people was as much as Miriam could bear. She couldn't survive losing anyone else. So she stayed away from anyone who even hinted at making a move.

Though she grew up there, Miriam had no close relatives left in Romania. To call those she still had distant would be an understatement. Her parents had been estranged from the rest of the family, on both sides, and Miriam was even more so.

Miriam's relatives were overwhelmed when her parents died within two months of each other. Her distant aunts (and uncles along with them) sent her from one city to another in the hope that another cousin would take her in.

So as soon as Miriam was eighteen and allowed to, she went to earn some money waitressing and delivering mail, and later found a small room at a student residence in Iasi, where none of her relatives lived. Three years later, having saved enough money from her multiple jobs and studied at the local university, she applied for the first overseas study opportunity she found, and moved to Aalborg.

She'd never heard of the city before and wouldn't even have known which country it was in.

The room she was sitting in now, was in the same apartment she'd found and rented shortly after moving to Denmark. She remembered how excited she had been to share it with just one girl of her age. The apartment was tiny, with floors and walls that vibrated when a truck or bus drove by, but it was a stone's throw from the city center, and it was more than big enough for the two young women.

The little apartment only got too crowded when Will visited Lily. Miriam didn't like those times. But Lily said she was in heaven having her two favorite people around her.

And now Lily was gone, and Will was coming to Aalborg on some business or other.

Why did he need her help anyway? He said she was the only friend in Aalborg he had left.

Friend?

Miriam had never considered herself Will's friend. True, they had been friendly when they first met at the language school, on a Danish course for internationals who'd moved to Aalborg. But when Miriam invited Lily to a party and she met Will, her flatmate soon started leaving the apartment to meet him, and Miriam's dislike began.

The dislike peaked when he made Lily's cancer all about him.

Oh well, I can't take it back, she thought of the "Yes" she had given Will, and tore herself off the sofa, relaxing the hand that was still clutching her phone.

After setting her mobile down in the charger, Miriam returned to her computer and thought about drafting a post for her blog. But her mind went blank. She didn't even know what topic to write about. Although her thoughts kept returning to the crazy idea she'd had shortly after Lily's death, to write a book about their friendship.

But Miriam didn't write books. That was reserved for people with more patience. Besides, writing about Lily would open too many wounds, which still hadn't fully healed. A memoir would require her to tell the story of her parents, and how she had come to Denmark. And maybe the fact that Lily was adopted, and how she'd felt growing up, not looking the same as her Danish parents and the children at school. That would require permission from Lily's parents, disturbing them in their grief. She couldn't do that.

Miriam sighed and opened several windows on social media. On the professional one, she typed Will's name, wondering why she was doing it since he would see that she had looked him up. Yeah, Miriam thought, you should know that I'm checking up on you.

Miriam discovered that Will was the founder of a little company in the UK that tested wheelchairs. It surprised her that Will could run a company. But the picture of him sitting on such a chair with a wide grin and thumbs up reinforced her dislike. What a hypocrite! It was fair enough that he ran such a company, but didn't it make fun of disabled people, to pose on a wheelchair when he was able-bodied, and even use it as his official profile image?

Miriam shook her head and decided to check her e-mails.

There was only one e-mail, from an address she didn't recognize: blogger@gamefulwriting.com.

She wanted to delete it or mark it as SPAM, but something stopped her. The sound of the domain name and the sheer idea of bringing games and writing together in one phrase caught her attention.

The text was harmless, too, except there was a link to www.gamefulwriting.com/blog/post1.

The previous December she'd been the victim of a phishing scam, and the anger still lingered. She had ordered something online and was waiting for it to arrive when she got a text from the courier service requesting fifteen kroner to deliver the package. It wasn't a lot of money, and though the tracking number was slightly wrong, she took it for a typo. So, she paid, entering her credit card details in the form she was taken to.

Shortly after, Miriam got two e-mails thanking her for subscribing to online services she'd never heard of (one of them for music). She quickly cancelled one subscription but was unable to cancel the other. The e-mail address provided didn't exist. To be sure, Miriam checked the domain name of the courier service that had asked for money and found an article about it in the Danish media. It was a scam used by criminals to steal people's money amidst the euphoria of Christmas shopping. As recommended by the article, Miriam called her bank and discovered the bandits had taken thirty times more than the fifteen kroner she'd agreed to pay. The only option she had was to block her bank card and order another. She'd have to do without the card she usually used.

So now she wasn't going to click blindly on a random link. She would check it out first.

She did. Several web-address review services evaluated the page as reputable and not affiliated to any other service. There wasn't a lot of traffic, but the reviewers praised the page for the many resources it provided. The page had existed since June 2014, and the design seemed unchanged since then. There were some complaints about the missing blog, but a note indicated it was to begin in January 2020. The general tone was very positive, praising a tremendous collection of uplifting and valuable resources in multiple formats, on writing and more.

Miriam recalled the link in the e-mail she'd just received. She returned to her e-mail program and sure enough, the text indicated quite clearly that the first blog post was at www.gamefulwriting.com/blog/post1.

Still a little reluctant to click on the link, Miriam returned to her browser and decided to check the site first. She found all the resources the positive reviews had referred to.

There were all kinds of references on the writing craft, but in addition were separate areas for books, articles, and podcasts on three other main topics.

The first of these was the art of living in the moment, and how to be truly present. There were some specific resources on mindfulness and anthropology too.

The second was kaizen. Miriam hadn't encountered the term before, but some brief scrolling and reading of summaries revealed it was about taking tiny steps towards your goals, solving big challenges in little bits, and awarding yourself small, consistent rewards. Somehow the first and second of these were appealing and made sense.

The third topic covered all things gameful. Some of the books listed were on gamification and serious games. Miriam hadn't heard of these before either. The summary below the title of the section was again helpful. It explained that gamification was about bringing game design elements into real-life situations and contexts. The list of examples made total sense: progress bars, stars for reviews, loyalty programs in coffee and other shops, language learning apps, and so many more. Miriam was pleasantly surprised by the serious games too. Many examples were about bringing awareness to critical issues such as vaccination, life as a refugee, domestic violence, fighting cancer, and so much more.

There was a long list of links to all kinds of games. The title of this subsection was "Games that Bring Joy."

Miriam immediately thought of Lily and Will. Both were avid gamers and loved playing on Lily's console in her room. Miriam wasn't really attached to video games, so was often left alone in the kitchen while they played, rolling about with laughter in Lily's room. The three of them did play board or card games occasionally, but more often than not, the video games prevailed. Miriam envied Will for having that part of Lily to himself.

She was jealous of Lily too. Why couldn't she, Miriam, find someone to love like Will? She had a boyfriend in Romania once and expected to marry him, though his mother wasn't in favor of the idea, trying to convince him they were too young. Which they were really, given they'd been just twenty at the time. But Miriam was blind to all reason, believing feelings to be absolute, and that once you had them, they would last forever. Well, of course, it had turned out differently than she'd thought. Her boyfriend kissed another girl right in front of her at a party. Faced with Miriam's anger, he just said, "Relax, have fun. Go and kiss someone. There are enough boys around."

So, she kept an eye out for handsome men, of any age, who were serious relationship material. So far, she hadn't found any.

But Lily seemed different. She didn't have one-night stands but she dated many young men, sometimes several in one week, and had enormous fun with it until, as she once expressed, only Will remained. Apparently he was the only one she could be herself with. Miriam couldn't fathom why.

Miriam looked down at her hand hovering over her computer mouse, and tried to tear her thoughts away from Lily and Will. Damn this, Will! Why did he have to call and remind her about Lily? Miriam sighed. Well, in truth, Miriam often thought of Lily. Living in this same apartment was a constant reminder, despite having refurbished Lily's room and now only using it for storage. The kitchen and living room were the worst.

Miriam rolled her shoulders and pressed "About" on the Gameful Writing site. To her surprise, this page contained only one sentence:

Please refer to the blog.

Well, all right, thought Miriam. Show me what you've got. She clicked on the flashing star labeled "Blog" and discovered the page announcing that the blog would go live in January 2020, with one blog post listed — the same she had got in her mailbox. She clicked the link to it and read.

✳✳

Welcome to the Gameful Writing Blog, and post number one, or Level One of your writing game, if you will. For, you guessed correctly, here we will be bringing games and writing together. Or in other words, we will address different kinds of writing (or at least those I can think of) in a fun, gameful way.

When I say "kinds of writing" I don't mean, for example, "academic" or "fiction," but rather classifications based on how we feel or think about them.

<u>First</u> of all we have the books or stories we want to write but fear the outcome of.

<u>Second</u> are the articles, reports, or other pieces we need to write but fret over the feedback we might get.

<u>Third</u>, the pieces we have committed to writing, but which we neither want nor consider it necessary to write. Oh, all you test and thesis writers, I hear you!

<u>Fourth</u> is writing to explore yourself, to find the truth in what you do. It is about finding the answer for why you chose to do something.

And don't forget the <u>fifth</u>, which is writing as a gift. I can't be the only person to wonder what to write in a birthday or Christmas card, or heaven forbid, when sitting down to write a letter! There's more to this type of writing, but please bear with me.

Believe it or not, embarking on this Gameful Writing adventure feels to me like a mixture of all five types. There may be more, or these could be divided into sub-types, but this is how I am able to sort my feelings about writing for now. I hope you can reflect on the classification above.

I have decided to remain anonymous for a couple of blog posts (probably five, you will see why later on). I will reveal a bit about myself in each, until you either solve the puzzle, or I introduce myself in the fifth or sixth post. You can choose to see this adventure as a puzzle or any other type of game that you like.

That is what this blog is ultimately about, and life too, if you will. It is about the way we choose to perceive what comes our way in each moment, and what we do with it.

You might ask what moved me to start this project. There are many, many reasons, but mainly because I love to read, and I love to play games.

Recently I also discovered my love for writing, and more precisely writing freely — letting whatever is boiling in my head spill over onto the screen through my keyboard, or a notebook through my pen.

I tried to pin down my preferred writing format, but struggled. Looking at what I most enjoy reading and playing revealed the answer.

I consume anything that is written, be it hardback or paperback, e-book, online article, blog post on social media, or even an ad on a milk carton. Also fiction, non-fiction, poetry, and anything else.

The same is true of games. Video, on a computer, tablet, or console, board, card, dice, sports, pranks with friends. Really, anything.

But I do have a thumbs-up and thumbs-down criterion. And this is, whatever I read or play should feel fun. I determine to devote my full attention to these creations, and I am willing to have fun (plus I love trying out new games), but if I or the other players don't feel uplifted, empowered, and entertained, then I leave those games be.

I apply the same criteria to what I write. This includes the things no one will ever see, as I write, smile over, and then throw them away, and others, such as this baby of mine, which I've allowed out into the world to meet you.

I decided to choose the blog format for this writing project because I can create and release each bit of it quickly. I am a gamer, so as soon as I reach one level, I want to try out the next one.

But let's start with the first level of our writing game: the books or stories we want to write, but are afraid of for some reason. What can help in this situation?

Firstly, becoming aware of your wish. Allowing yourself to have it. How do you do that, you ask?

Do it like an anthropologist would, when studying an interesting culture. You are a fascinating culture of one, exposed to many fascinating collective cultures, absorbing and mixing and sometimes boiling those juices into a very personal cocktail.

Let's look at it together. Just think, would you admit to yourself that you wanted to play a certain game? You might not begin playing it the very moment you think of it, but you wouldn't fight the desire to do so. You might, instead, allow yourself time to play it. Many of us relax with a round of Candy Crush Saga, Sudoku, or Minesweeper.

So why not allow yourself the wish to write a book, article or poem, and let yourself relax into testing and playing (with) it?

You can do it in your downtime, or just for fun.

Even if your writing project has some bigger purpose, like to serve someone you love or to support yourself financially, don't load it with drama. You wouldn't stake your entire well-being on a game of Candy Crush. The combination of all your choices contribute to your well-being, from one moment to the next. Right now you might be amused by reading this blog (at least I hope so), later playing a board game with your children or a friend, and then a round of writing your book or blog post.

Again, like in a game, you might momentarily resent hitting a blank page or line (wall) on your keyboard (with your car in a racing game), but then you can immediately search for a quick solution. In a car racing game, you would reverse and continue down the road. In writing, you could go back to the last moment of fun and flow and take another turn from there.

So, don't put too much pressure on the writing game to make you or someone else happy or rich. Because if you do, you will prevent yourself from having fun while testing and playing it.

Instead, start playing. In other words, write.

That is what I am doing right now. I am playing my blog writing game, Level One (because it is the first blog post), and I utterly enjoy it.

For you, my writing game, or at least this level of my writing game, will be in the past, and instead, you will find yourself playing the reading game.

And you are doing it brilliantly, if you've come this far and are reading these words. A few more pages and you will get your first Gameful Reading Badge for reading this post to the end.

The next step would be to play a game where you can earn your first Gameful Writing Badge, by playing a round of your writing game and finishing it.

Before I help you set the rules for your writing game, let me set a few things straight. You are the co-designer of this game. You can't put the entire responsibility for your game on me. You have to do your part in its design, since we are talking about the writing elements of your life, not mine. I am playing my game now, so it's progressing for me. Right now, you are learning how to play this game by looking over another player's shoulder — mine, in this case — by reading this blog post. After that, you'll go and design and play your writing game.

Having established that, here's what else you can expect from the Gameful Writing Blog. I will post once a month. That is how long I want to give myself and you to reach our gameful writing levels.

I'll be playing my writing game daily if I can, but in-between I will be playing other games too. Games in their classical sense, but also the games of reading and learning, the online surfing game, cooking, sleeping, waking up, and whatever else life demands of me (which are always surprising) games, as well.

So, once a month, you can expect me to introduce another level of our writing game, or in other words, a blog post on the next writing type of those outlined above.

But, whichever writing type struck a chord with you the most as you read the list, here's the simplest way to play the writing game.

1. Prepare all the gadgets you need to play your writing game.

Here are mine: a notebook and a functioning ballpoint pen (it has to be a ballpoint pen for me!), other times also my laptop, a timer or a timer app on my mobile, a notepad to record my points and draw my stars and badges, a glass of water, a cup of espresso (not every time). Sometimes a small square of chocolate to go with the coffee.

Here are some more ideas for gadgets, which I don't use, but you might find useful: a tablet if you prefer or can write longhand on it, a dictating app on your tablet or mobile, a note app on your mobile, a scrap of paper if you don't want to use a notepad for your points, a Microsoft Excel spreadsheet for your score or word count (which is a score in itself), or an app you find or create for recording your rewards. And of course, your favorite drink. But don't use alcohol. The thrill of mindful writing will be enough to make you jitter with excitement.

I think this is more or less it. Oh, sometimes, I use colorful and glittery stickers as the badges in my personal Leaderboard Book.

If you wonder why I call it a Leaderboard while being the only player, then here's the reason. My driving self plays against the part of me that puts the breaks on. You could say I organize Olympic games for them. Instead of fighting and calling each other names, the creative and procrastinating parts of me play peaceful, fun games. So if I have a maximum number of points to allocate, like a total number of points a day (if you give yourself one point for every ten minutes then you can collect one hundred and forty-four points in every twenty-four hours), then at the beginning or end of a day I can see who got how many of these maximum number of points.

2. *The next step is to choose or let luck decide how much time you want to invest in your writing game round, or writing sprint as some writers call it.*

I often limit my writing sprints or rounds to five or ten minutes at most. But here is what I meant by letting luck decide the number of minutes. That would be a variant of this game round, if you will. I will try to come up with a new option for this game during each round to keep it fun. And maybe inspire you to come up with your unique variants.

So, here is the playful variant this time. Take a dice (or more than one, if you want to write for longer), or open a dice app online and roll the dice. You can also decide to ignore one or other of the small numbers and roll again. Or total all the points after rolling three times, or add those on the multiple dice, if you play (yes, this is part of the game too!) with more than one at a time. It is your choice. But when you have rolled the number of times you decided (you could also determine this number with a roll of the dice, just once I would say ;)), then set your timer to this time and play.

Here is another idea: you can choose that the number you roll is how many sentences you must write in this round. Choose whatever feels best (or most fun) for you. The only mistake you can make is not giving it a try. I am super glad that I did.

But if you are still scared to start writing, even for the shortest time or a single sentence, here are a few ideas. You might have heard about freewriting, whereby you spill out onto the page whatever comes to mind on the topic you want or need to write about. It is a great possibility.

But here's another. At this stage, you don't even have to write whole sentences. You can start with bullet points or even the sentence, "I have no idea where this will go." Or "I am scared to death." Or "I hope no one will ever,

29

ever see this." Whatever you write, just put those words down. You'll be surprised by what follows, I promise. And especially by the feeling you have when the timer goes off.

By the way, if you want to play another round of the writing game, just put on the timer (or roll the dice before that) and write.

3. When you finish your round of writing, you get your first Gameful Writing Badge. I invite you to draw the most beautiful badge you can for it, on a scrap of paper or your Points and Badges Leaderboard. A reminder: if you don't write on any given day, then the badge for that day goes to your procrastinating self, who also does his or her best to win.

Go ahead and announce your win (both Reading and Writing badges) in the comments below. Don't forget to share the rules you decide upon with others. And also, how many game rounds you played before stopping or, in other words, how many Gameful Writing Badges you collected for Level One, because you collect a badge for each successful writing round or sprint. But leave some of them for the following days before round two. Don't overload yourself, simply have fun.

Remember, FUN is your compass. Always have it handy.

I won't respond because I will be busy playing my games, whatever and wherever they might be, but go ahead and cheer each other on.

I've configured the comments in such a way that you will remain anonymous, and you will see "Comment 4," for example, appearing across your comment after posting it, if you are the fourth person to report your wins. And if you comment separately about your reading and writing badges, then you will have two comment numbers. So, if you want to point out in "Comment 8" that you also wrote "Comment 4," then go ahead and do so. You are welcome to reveal who you are in the comments but I wanted to give you the option of remaining anonymous, as I have (at least for the time being).

Remember, all this is about having fun while letting yourself live up to your dreams.

Now, do you have all your gadgets ready? Yes?

Then on my count: ready, set, go!

***

Miriam stared at the screen in front of her. Then she stood up, went to her little kitchen, opened the lowest drawer, and took out a dice cup with six dice that she hadn't touched since she last played with Lily and Will so many years ago. She left five of the dice on the counter and returned to her desk.

She rolled and got six. Of course, she smiled to herself, surprised to find she was happy at the thought of writing for more rather than less time. She took out her mobile and set the timer app to six minutes. Then she opened her text editor, started a new document, and briefly stopped. She got up again and fetched herself a glass of water.

She couldn't help but grin at how seriously, no, not seriously, but diligently, she was following the recommendation of an unknown blogger and how lightly it appeared to begin a project she had so wanted and dreaded in the past.

Miriam breathed out. Let's start the game.

When the timer went off, she looked at the word count at the bottom of the editor window. Three hundred and two words. Wow! In six minutes!?

The text was a mess. Bullet points, sentences.

But one thing was clear. A story was emerging. A fictional story. About two young women from different parts of the world meeting and helping each other through the most challenging times. And although the story was far from a comedy, Miriam couldn't help but grin! She'd had so much fun during those six minutes.

Wait, was she allowed to have fun with all the grief she had to bear? Fear jumped up in her again. But something had changed, and another voice within her asked, is it fear or excitement at where this might lead? I wonder how much I will manage to write by the second round of Gameful Writing next month.

There was another overall feeling too. As she wondered, Miriam began to get excited about the following days and next month. Not fearing them, but being curious. She no longer regretted saying "yes" to Will. Now she could even admit to herself that she wanted to see him again. It might heal some wounds, or at least give her the chance to tell him what she thought of him. She hadn't managed to do it when Lily died. But even this thought was not heavy. She needed to let the author of the blog know (even though they said they would not be answering the comments) what this ten-minute read, and the subsequent six-minute writing exercise had done for her.

She opened the browser window with the blog post and typed her comment:

It is crazy, and I can't believe it, but I just earned both the Gameful Reading and Gameful Writing Badges in this round. And it was for the first writing type that the blogger defined.

I've wanted to write a book for so long, but I didn't know where to start and have fretted about its shape and form. And this silly (sorry for calling it silly; without your brilliant post, I would never have done it) exercise and 302 words opened up something I could never have fathomed. Good luck to all the players. I'm excited to discover what will happen in the following rounds of this game.

After pressing "Post comment," the screen refreshed, and she discovered that hers was the sixth comment. Six was also the number she had rolled on the dice before writing. She had to smile at this coincidence. Somehow it felt like good luck.

Miriam gasped, realizing that she had opened up her feelings in a comment on an anonymous page to the whole world. Just like that. She chuckled and scrolled up to read all the comments before hers.

The first five comments echoed her feelings, and two had pictures of their self-drawn badges. One was quite intricate. Miriam vaguely recalled that this technique was called doodling or something. She'd check that later.

Oh, Miriam thought and realized that she'd completely forgotten to record her win and give herself a badge. After a short contemplation she became aware that she didn't want to draw her reward. She went to the bookshelf, where she kept a small chest containing semi precious stones. She took out a small leather pouch and wrote on the label with washing instructions, "Miriam's Writing Game," then put a green stone with red streaks into the pouch. Then she took a picture of this small composition and posted it in the comment, which happened to be comment number nine:

Commenter 6 here. I rolled the dice and got six. Strangely instead of being frightened, I was glad to get the chance to write for a longer time. I wrote for six minutes. My badge is this semi precious stone. I have a whole collection of these stones, which I stopped adding to and looking at a while ago. Now they will serve as badges for the rounds of my writing game. (By the way, it feels great owning (designing and playing) this game!) I will keep the stones in this pouch and will share with you how many I collect before the next round. Happy winning to all!

Miriam refreshed the screen afterwards several times, revelling in the wordless "trance," she felt after what had just happened. With each refresh, she saw more comments appearing, reporting successes and responding to hers, congratulating her on the brilliant idea of the stones.

But what echoed from all of them was that they all felt like winners.

Miriam couldn't believe that just a couple of hours ago she had felt miserable and now… Wow.

Now, she wasn't miserable. Strangely, she felt in control. She had an appetite for playing the writing game. She also realized that she wanted to blog about it now. Writing her blog now felt like a game of its own, a different one, but still a writing game. So, she opened her website, pressed "New Blog Post," and wrote:

I need to share something amazing with you while the feeling is fresh. And after that, I will go back to the game I just played. But before I do that, I would like to share with you this blog post, about which I got notified today.

She copied and pasted the link to the Gameful Writing post number one. And added:

I won't try to interpret what is said there. I will just tell you that I was very suspicious of the e-mail in my Inbox, having recently walked into a phishing trap (as I reported several posts back — check here). But after checking that the page was reputable and even recommended for its brilliant collection for writers, even if a little outdated, I went and read the first blog post, which I share with you here. Reading it changed my day. And probably my whole month too. If not more. I won't keep you from reading it any longer. Just go there and read, and it might change your perspective and your actions too. If you are wondering which of the comments are mine, look out for the comments 6 and 9. No more spoilers. Now, go and read. And I will get back to my game.

And she did just that.

Chapter 2: Will

*

Will rolled through customs, the pretty airport attendant right behind him with his case.

He saw Miriam immediately. Her hair was longer than five years back. He remembered how Miriam and Lily used to have their hair cut the same length. Lily's black and straight and Miriam's almost as black but in waves. He chuckled at the memory that flashed up. He had accompanied both women to a new salon once, and Miriam had actually admonished the hairdresser for cutting hers a couple of centimeters shorter than Lily's.

Right now, Miriam's hair was flowing to half cover her shoulders as she intently scanned the crowd exiting security at the arrivals in Aalborg airport.

Then she noticed him as he rolled towards her in his wheelchair. She frowned, and her face quickly displayed a mixture of confusion and surprise. "Oh, hi, um."

"Hi, Miri." He didn't know what to say either.

He felt a movement behind him. The attendant behind cleared her throat and said, "Are you all right now, or do you need any more help?"

Will turned to look at the attendant as she moved to his side and stopped to look at him. Will turned to Miriam. "Um."

Miriam was seemingly waking from the awkwardness between the three of them. "I'll take it." She reached for Will's case.

The attendant wished them a good day and walked briskly away.

Will turned his chair but didn't know what to do next. "Shall we…"

"Um… Look, Will, I didn't know you were…"

Will looked up. "I thought you knew. Sorry for not telling you explicitly. I guess my request for help was not that clear. I might need a larger taxi to transport me. But maybe that attendant can help me?"

"Look, Will, I said I would help you, and I will." He saw annoyance in her eyes. But then she took a deep breath and said something he didn't expect. "I just need a moment to recover from the news. They have good coffee and pastries here at the airport since they renovated it. Do you care to sit down? Um, I mean to get a coffee or something and talk a little."

"That would be lovely." He saw a frown on Miriam's face like he was someone she didn't recognize at all. And he couldn't blame her for that. He gestured toward the hallway, down which the airport attendant had disappeared. "This way?"

"Yes," Miriam said and moved aside to give him space to turn and follow.

They each paid for their own coffees and desserts in the airport cafe, and Will transported their tray on his lap. Miriam found them a small table and moved a chair out of the way to accommodate Will's wheelchair. She took the tray to arrange their food and drinks, then settled across from him. After sipping their coffees and nibbling the cinnamon snails Will hadn't eaten in the five years since he'd left Denmark, he finally gathered all his courage, looked up and said, "Miri—"

"What happened?" Miriam glanced at the wheelchair and then back at him.

"It was…" Will almost said "an accident," the fable he and his family had been telling for five years. But something stopped him. It almost felt like lying to Lily, and he couldn't do that anymore, especially not to the memory of her. He sighed. "I…, I tried to kill myself, and it didn't quite work out. The bridge I jumped from at the railway station was too low, and the track I fell on annoyingly wasn't in use that day." Despite his best efforts he never managed to make it sound funny, and he tried often enough, whenever his parents or brothers broached the topic. He braced himself for a blunt look from Miriam.

"Was it higher or lower than the one at the main station in Aalborg?" Miriam asked.

"Huh?"

"The railway bridge."

Will caught a glimpse of amusement in Miriam's eyes as she took her cup and sipped at her espresso while eyeing him over the cup's edge. Will found himself smiling too. So the joke had worked. For the first time. He let out a chuckle. "Lower. I wasn't even knocked out, not even with all the booze in my blood. It hurt like hell until the paramedics came."

"Your mother said you went into rehab when she came to pick up your things."

"I know. Thanks for helping my mum out, and sorry for not thanking you until now. I was ashamed. My mum was ashamed then too. So, she spread that thing about rehab whenever someone asked where I was. And it wasn't that far from the truth. The hospital was pretty similar to rehab. I haven't had a drop of alcohol since. And not because I'm afraid of getting in that state again. There's no point for it now." Will turned the cup in his hands around its axis.

"There wasn't a point then either."

Will looked at Miriam. She was right, and there was no point in explaining and trying to defend himself. "No, there wasn't. I'm sorry."

"I miss her. And your call a month ago reminded me how much I do."

"I miss her too. I know it sounds strange, but I felt like my injuries brought me closer to her." He clasped his cup stronger, hearing how stupid that sounded. "Sorry, this is stupid."

"It is." Miriam smiled.

"I wanted to ask you something…" Will stopped, unsure how to continue.

"Yes?"

Will didn't know Miriam had so much patience in her. She would let him finish his question. "Would you go to the cemetery, to Lily's grave, with me? It's been over five years since she died, and I wanted to go there."

"I thought you didn't remember when you called me."

"I know you didn't believe in my feelings for her, but I did love her."

"I know, I'm sorry."

Will shook his head, unsure at what. "I'm sorry too. It was the anniversary of her death that prompted me to organize all these meetings I have this week. And also why I called you. I wanted to meet and apologize."

"Well, it's too late now." Miriam snapped then sighed. "No, it's not too late. Sorry. It's good that you did it. It feels like closure in a way. Not completely, but at least a little bit."

Will nodded. He never felt at ease with Miriam before, especially not after she introduced him to Lily. But today was different. What a common loss could do. "I started following your blog and saw the post on gamefulwriting.com. You are right. It's quite fun."

"Yes, strangely, it changed so much for me. Even my resentment toward you has changed. And I had it before Lily got sick." Miriam frowned. "I don't know why I'm telling you this now. Sorry, it's out of place."

Will smiled and waved Miriam's apology away. "No problem." He sipped his coffee and said, "I signed up to your blog several days before calling you and saw you'd written the post a couple of hours after we talked. So you discovered the writing game that same day?"

"Yes, I discovered it right after you called me. I swore at myself for agreeing to help you, and then discovered the blog post, read it, and admitted that I wanted to. Lily would want me to." She paused. "I always wanted to write a book about Lily and myself, and the friendship we had, but never dared. I started right after reading the post." Miriam frowned. "I can't believe I am telling you this. You are the first person to know about me writing this book. Don't tell anyone."

"I won't. But you are not the first to reveal a secret today. You are the first person besides my family to know the truth about why I am paralyzed from the waist down."

"Oh." Miriam studied him. "Wait. Are you by any chance billythebrokensoul@mail.co.uk?"

Will supported himself on his chair's armrests and shifted in his chair. It was always his tactic to avoid eye contact, but Miriam waited for him to answer, so he looked back at her. "Yes, how did you guess? You must have many subscribers every day."

"Well, not every day but quite a few each month. But that address stuck with me, and now, after what you just told me, plus the 'co.uk' extension, it was easy to guess."

"I guess it was." Will picked up his fork, cut a piece of pastry snail and put it in his mouth. He feared the same discussion he had with his mother. It was just his private address, which Will usually used when he wanted to remain anonymous. But he had to admit that for those who knew him, it wasn't that anonymous, as Miriam had just confirmed.

"You should change it," Miriam said, interrupting his thoughts. "It's strange, but I only now see that Lily was right."

Now it was Will's turn to frown. "About what?"

"Sometime before her death, the hospital personnel walked you out for being too loud and too drunk. I stayed with Lily, and I ranted about you. But she said that your behavior was just punishing yourself. I thought you were an arrogant prick. Sorry." Miriam smiled apprehensively. "But that was what I thought. Even one month ago, after you called and I checked your profile, I still couldn't stop thinking that way. I was impressed that you were the founder of a company that served people with disabilities. But I saw the photograph of you sitting in the wheelchair, grinning, with your thumbs up, and I assumed you were an even bigger hypocrite than I thought. You were sitting there in a wheelchair while being fully able to walk. It didn't even enter my mind that something might have happened to you that made the wheelchair necessary. I felt quite stupid when I finally saw you approaching me just now."

Miriam took her fork, cut a piece of her cinnamon roll, forked it, but didn't eat it. She put the fork down and looked again at Will. "Now I see with everything that happened afterward and this e-mail address that she was right. Stop it, OK?" Miriam put her forearms on the table and leaned toward him. "Do you know what I will do if you don't change the address in the next seven days? OK, OK." She raised her hands, palms facing him. "Two weeks."

"What?" Will somehow felt his mood lifting instead of feeling threatened. He smiled.

"I will block your e-mail address or even declare it as SPAM."

"You wouldn't!" Will grinned, not quite believing that he and Miriam were joking with each other.

"I would, and I will. You have two weeks and not a minute longer."

"All right, all right. I'll see what I can do. Do you have a tip for the new e-mail address?"

"What's wrong with your name?"

Will chuckled. "Nothing." Miriam was always very blunt and straight with what she thought. Five years back, he resented it. But not now. Now, he admitted, he liked it very much.

**

The week in Aalborg passed too quickly.

Miriam didn't have time to meet him in the city during his stay, except for the one time they went together to Lily's grave. They didn't talk much, only really exchanging words when Miriam needed instruction to get his wheelchair to roll on the churchyard gravel. She also placed the flowers he bought for Lily in the vase beside the headstone. Although they didn't talk much with each other, Will was utterly aware that Miriam's presence made this visit less of a burden, especially when she patted him on the shoulder while he was trying to hide the tears and dabbed with his palms at his eyes.

The rest of his stay was busy because he had a social event with the wheelchair community in Aalborg, a visit and subsequent dinner with the local wheelchair repair service he had discovered some time ago and wanted to exchange experience with, a day at the hospital meeting patients who had just started using a wheelchair, and especially those who had to face the long-term use of them, as he did. He also found a great little company where he could purchase quality spare parts for his business at a fair price. This small company even had a flexible plan outlined for collaboration with British companies after BREXIT. They did business globally as well and could show Will how they planned to make the transition from current handling with Great Britain to after BREXIT was finalized, and also for different scenarios of its outcome. He couldn't believe his luck. Something drew him to Aalborg. Well, it was somebody. It was a person who no longer lived there, no longer lived at all. But her spirit still did. And he felt this through his whole stay, especially during those personal meetings, outside of his business schedule.

First, while meeting with Miriam, of course, but then also meeting and apologizing to the medical personnel at the department of oncology at the hospital. They didn't hold any grudge against him, although they remembered him well, even after all those years and the many patients, family members and friends they had encountered since. One of the doctors guessed why he was in the chair without saying it directly, with everyone understanding what he meant. Will found himself reaching for the assorted chocolates he'd brought as a gift for the doctors and nurses, and before he could stop himself, he shoveled one into his mouth and nodded. He couldn't lie when someone asked so directly, although at the same time indirectly. He earned a pat on his right arm and a slap on his left shoulder simultaneously for his nod.

They talked about Lily and recalled her sweet jokes and the magic tricks she played on the personnel, which were always kind and joyful and never made anyone angry. A nurse mentioned the little colorful origami butterflies appearing magically on a tray after Lily had a meal, with "Thank you" written in small, round letters on their wings, and a doctor recalled how a red foam clown nose appeared in his hand after he shook Lily's hand during one of the visits. She did all that almost until the day she died. When complimented and asked how she got the idea for her sweet deeds, she often shrugged and said, "I once looked up online what volunteers do at the hospitals to brighten the day of cancer patients, and I thought, why can't I as a patient do the same to brighten the day of those who help me?"

Another nurse surprised everyone in the personnel room, where they had coffee with Will, by taking one of Lily's butterflies out of her wallet and showing it around. She looked both melancholic and at peace when she said, "It always reminds me how a small gesture can make a big difference." After everyone present took a look at the pink origami butterfly, gingerly holding and passing it from one to another (Will was permitted to have it longest), the nurse put it carefully back into her wallet.

Yes, the week in Aalborg, which he was dreading before the trip, turned out to be a very special week, healing many wounds.

Miriam came to the airport to say good-bye, and they agreed to stay in touch and to meet again when Will returned on business. Will hoped it would be soon.

Now, two days after his return from Aalborg, he became aware of how eagerly he awaited the second Gameful Writing blog post. It was due today.

He was ashamed to admit to Miriam that when he got the notification about the blog post, he clicked the link immediately without checking the authenticity of the site. So, he didn't tell Miriam about getting the blog announcement from the Gameful Writing blogger at all. Worse still was that he had clicked on the link while at work. In doing so he had risked crashing his company's IT system again. He'd done it once before by clicking on a link that had infected all three servers with an intractable virus. George, the head of IT, was not happy. Clicking on gamefulwriting.com might have led to another such case. Luckily for Will, it hadn't.

The first blog post didn't quite address him, because it was about writing something you wanted to. Will didn't have anything against writing, but it was more that he needed to learn the art of it than that it was his passion. The aspect of his work he loved most was testing or coordinating the tests by others of various equipment for those who needed to use a wheelchair or wear prosthetics. He loved getting more and more testers for his team and seeing their happy faces when he offered them a paid job to test equipment for those who were in the same situations as themselves. Inclusivity Testing Repair & Upgrade (ITRU Ltd.) was his pride and passion. And his parents' too. Especially his mum's, who took over the HR and bookkeeping tasks in their company. His dad was a board member and helped where he could.

So, working with his hands, repairing, upgrading, helping to repair, and finding new ways of doing things while sitting in a wheelchair, was both rewarding and fun. Writing was a necessary tool for Will as the company's CEO and founder, to spread news about the company and also to lead it. They were growing every year, and he now needed to write memos every day, both internal and those open to the public, and to multiple people and personnel.

He didn't have any problem with that, as long as the memo was not about him. He still hadn't revealed the reason for his own wheelchair to his co-workers.

He had lied to them for the company's three year existence. OK, to some of those who joined later, it had been less than three years. But did that really count? Will didn't think so. He was too ashamed to reveal the actual reason, and now he was embarrassed that he had lied.

But shame didn't help. To Will's surprise, he discovered that opening up about his suicide attempt felt healing. Talking to Miriam about it and her reaction, as well as their continued correspondence, gave him an idea of what could happen if he opened up. He chuckled now at the recent memory of deleting his "broken soul" e-mail address immediately upon reaching his hotel room. He let Miriam know that he had subscribed with his business address, which contained his full name and concluded with the acronym for the company. Since then (a little over a week ago), they had already exchanged several e-mails and personal messages on two social media platforms. He couldn't believe this turn of events.

But there was still something he hadn't managed to write yet. An account of his suicide attempt, for his colleagues, which could be made public. His mother was right; he needed to let them know. And the longer the company existed, the faster it grew, and the more who joined the team, the more urgent this message became.

His mother would do anything to help him tell his story, but she was right, she couldn't start it for him. He needed to take the first step. But how?

He hoped that the second Gameful Writing blog post would help him with that. The author said that he (or was it a she?) would talk today about the writing that one needed to do but was afraid of or resented doing.

Well, the blogger hadn't said that this topic would be discussed today, but this type of writing was listed as the second, so Will hoped it would be. And the blogger didn't say that he or she would publish the posts exactly one month apart. It could be one month and a couple of days.

But Will hoped it would be today. He suspected that he didn't only need to write it, but he now also wanted to, to take this load off his shoulders and put it down on paper. But how? Could a timer really help him?

Will was grateful for the distraction he'd had this morning. They had been working with the manufacturer to adapt one of the wheelchair models for use by rugby players, but there was a problem with the upgrade. Some of the rubber covers kept falling off, and the exposed metal parts underneath could be dangerous for the quickly moving players during a game. Will was super glad when the potential sub-contractor in Aalborg had a solution. They would use both special cutting techniques and 3D printers to produce intricate rubber and plastic parts. Will and the CEO of this company hadn't expected to work together that fast, but both were happy to do so.

Now, back in his office, he sat in front of his computer for a few seconds, telling himself not to be disappointed if the blog post wasn't there yet.

But it was.

Will clicked on the link in the notification and started to read.

***

The second post wasn't that different to the first, except it was shorter, and it indeed concentrated on the second type of writing defined by the blogger. Those things we need to write but fret over the feedback.

Will breathed out in relief as the text of the blog post struck a chord.

Welcome to the second Gameful Writing blog post, or Level Two of your writing game!

The first type of writing we discussed last time (check it out here) was more for those who love the process of writing.

This one is for those of you who think that you need to write something, but you don't know how. I discovered that when I felt this way, I didn't only need to write or express something. In truth, I wanted to do it, with all my heart, but simply was afraid to put it into words. I even dressed this fear into the sentence, "I don't know how to do it."

Then I heard a song with a lyric that really struck me. The line was about being guided by your conscience, without feeling any shame, and just telling your truth.

Amazing, right?

Well, this is what I did in parts of this blog, as well as in some recent e-mails and letters (yeah, even people my age write letters; A spoiler, or, you could say, revealing a piece of my puzzle: I'm young, what most consider young nowadays. I'm in my twenties).

Right now, you might be pushing against the door of truth to keep it hidden. But the truth and life in you are much stronger and more reliable than your fears. So stop pushing. Take the truth and life itself and their waterfall strength as allies. Crack the door open and see what happens. I'm grateful I did.

So, here is the solution for you to find the words. Put the timer on for however long you wish and play the writing game. I should say, play several rounds in a row by pressing start on your timer as soon as it goes off, and then tick your point or draft your badge.

I also promised to give you a new variant, for you to have a go at playing with the design of the writing game. This one uses a deck of cards (for example, with the standard fifty-two card deck or the fifty-four one with jokers). So, you shuffle the cards and then choose one at random. The number on it would mean the number of minutes or sentences to write. The face cards signify eleven, twelve, and thirteen points for jacks, queens, and kings respectively. The ace could be your pass or a gift-card for a ten-minute break or a cup of coffee or both. If you use the deck with jokers, then a joker could permit you to turn the remaining cards in the deck face up and choose whichever card you wish. (A tip: time this choice as well, so you don't end up jumping from one card to another. ;D)

You could also add meaning to the colors (or suits) of the cards. For example, if you get a card with clubs (♣), then this would mean outlining or brainstorming a new idea. Diamonds (♦) could be writing something new along that or another outline. Hearts (♥) could stand for free writing (without an outline), and spades (♠) editing or revising what you've written before.

Please, adjust this design to your preferences from one round to another.

Even if this blog post is shorter than the first one, I think I've said enough, and it's time for you to write and for me to take a break from writing. :D

Ready, set, go!

Will found himself smiling. He felt a calm spreading inside him. But he also had to shake his head in disbelief. Will couldn't believe that this phrase, the "writing game," just two words put together, could make his task so much easier to achieve. But he was willing to give it a try.

He didn't have a deck of cards at work, so he decided to take the blogger's five-minute average for his sprint. He opened a browser window on his computer and searched for an online timer. He made it small so that he could view both his text editor and the timer app at the same time. He was determined to write this time. OK, Will thought, the blogger said, start playing right away. So, let's play.

Will couldn't tell how much time had passed when his mother interrupted his writing by knocking and entering. She said she needed to inform him of the numbers on their profits and investments for the past month.

After they discussed their company's business, Mary, as they had agreed Will would call his mother at work, settled in a chair on the other side of Will's desk. Will saw her raising her eyebrows at a scrap of paper beside him with a tally, which had been hidden while they were discussing the company's expenses and revenue. Will followed her gaze and was surprised to see twelve points recorded on the tally. Will realized that he had written for a whole hour, or even more if he had forgotten to log one or other of his five-minute sprints.

He turned back to his mother and said, "Mum, I started writing the memo."

Mary nodded, and Will saw that he didn't need to explain to her what the memo was.

"I am almost done, in fact." Will looked at his screen and felt surprise that he had come so far in writing something he had resisted for so long. He turned back to his mother, "I will probably use several rounds to revise it myself, but I would be really grateful if you and dad could read it tonight and give me your feedback. I want to talk about it at the company meeting tomorrow, and I would like to send the memo out first thing in the morning."

His mother smiled. "Yes, absolutely. I will read it as soon as you send it to me and your father will surely do the same. But you said 'rounds.' What did you mean by that?"

Will laughed. "Did I use the word 'rounds'?" Upon his mother's amused nod, he said. "It's a writing game, which I discovered on a blog a month ago. I got a notification in my mailbox, but I have no idea from whom. The blogger is anonymous. I don't know why I got it. Maybe it was some kind of mistake, or maybe it's from someone here, who doesn't want to reveal themselves, or someone in Aalborg who knows my old university e-mail address there, the messages from which are still forwarded to this one at the company. Whoever might be behind this blog, the ideas there are great. Also, because they are so simple." He told Mary about the blog and the writing game. He also shared the variants with dice and cards.

"All right, send me the memo, and I will let you know how many five-minute rounds I use to read and comment on it." Mary's smile widened. "I'm competitive, you know, so I want to make it faster than your revision game. Don't forget to send me the statistics for your writing and revision games." Mary grinned. "I bet your father will be even more eager to win this."

Mary paused, changing her expression from smiling to one of concern. "I'm so glad you are laughing again, Will. Ever since Lily got her diagnosis and especially after her death, you've done it, smiling or laughing, I mean, rarely. I could probably count the times on one hand. But in the past month, I've heard you laughing more often. Maybe it is this game that's helped you with that, or maybe it was going to Aalborg. In the past two days, I've rarely seen you frowning."

Will turned the pen he didn't notice he had in his hands and nodded. "Yes, it was good to go there, to talk to Miriam and Lily's doctors at the hospital. I didn't manage to meet more people who knew Lily this time, but I hope I will next time. I plan to go to Aalborg more often in the future, with the new supplier and all."

Mary nodded and appeared pensive. "Are Lily's parents still in Aalborg?"

"I don't know. I was as scared, and probably still am, to contact Lily's parents as I was to write this memo. I didn't contact them. I didn't dare yet."

"You will don't worry. Look how much you managed this time. And I don't mean our company's business, but your heart's business. Contacting Miriam and going to the oncology department was a big step." Mary paused, then narrowed her eyes as if remembering something. "You just said you *were* afraid of writing the memo. You aren't anymore."

Even if his mother said the last sentence more as a statement than a question, Will felt that he still needed to nod his assent. Then he said, "I am still scared of the reaction towards it. But it feels like a whole load of dread has been left in the past, even if the very recent past. I can't believe what happened in the last hour, when I finally surrendered to write about my suicide attempt and what happened five years ago. It was so freeing. I am still scared to death of how everyone will react, but now I don't have any doubts that I have to, and I want to do it. If their reactions in any way resemble Miriam's reaction, then I will be the luckiest CEO and founder there is."

"You already are. Those who work here are the best team one could have, and they will support you all the way. You'll see. But I have another question to ask though. Will you make it public?"

Will nodded and was surprised by his confidence that he would do that. "I will send it in the morning as an internal memo, and then in the afternoon after the meeting, I will make it public on our blog."

"You're doing the right thing." Mary stood, went behind Will's chair, laid her hands on his shoulders, and kissed the top of his head. "I'm so proud of you. I know you don't want to hear it, but my readiness to be open about your story and my wish to help others in the same situation, especially parents like me, comes from what you've built with this company. I think you would have found a way to write this memo eventually, had you not discovered this Gameful Writing blog. But I see that it helped."

Will put his hand on his mother's and turned in his chair as much as he could to look at her. With a smile, he said, "It sure did."

Mary patted his hand and shoulders and came back to collect the folder she brought with her and leave. "You know, from what you told me, this blogger sounds so much like Lily. She was also playful, loved games, but was never careless and always present and attentive. I bet she would have loved the idea and found out who the blogger is. Lily rarely gave up on something she set her mind to. I wonder if she, I mean the blogger, ever reveals herself."

"Why do you think it is a woman?"

"I don't know, just a feeling. Or maybe just because the story you told me about the blog reminded me of Lily."

"You're right. It does sound very much like Lily. But the blogger started the blog only a month ago. So it couldn't have been Lily. The blogger promised to reveal who he or she is along with more of their story in the next few posts, by the fifth or sixth one at the latest."

"Good! Otherwise, I'd die waiting." Mary grunted, "And your father before me." Mary went to the door and turned, raising her right index finger in a lecturing manner. "Don't forget to send me the link to the blog and all your gaming statistics. Maybe we should spread this idea within the company. We could all use this gameful approach, not only for writing whatever we have to write for the business, but also for other daily tasks."

 She is right, Will thought as the door closed behind his mother. He jotted down the header "Memo for me:" in his notebook, and then made a note right after on another line:

Share the writing game and the Gameful Writing site with the company.

On another thought, he wrote:

Order timers, dice, card decks, and some board and other card games (e.g., UNO) for every location in the company. Warn Mum (Mary) that we might need to allocate regular expenses on these and other gameful gadgets, especially for refills. Ask her, the team leaders, and the board what they think of getting some of these gadgets made with the ITRU logo on them, to play within the company but also with guests and customers during breaks and social events, and have them as give-aways.

Chapter 3: Toni

*

At home, Toni leaned forward in his squeaky computer chair and threw a half-eaten piece of pizza into the box beside his computer.

"Damn it! I'm Italian and I'm eating pizza made by someone who's probably never been to Italy!"

It's not that the pizza was terrible. It wasn't. It was just different. Too many herbs somehow tasted out of place. Were these Herbs de Provence on a Pizza?! But other than that, and maybe if you called it a pie rather than a pizza, then it would be all right for a take out.

And it wasn't about the pizza anyway.

"What am I still doing here in this cold, dark corner of the world where March feels like January?" he demanded of his laptop, which looked patiently back at him. "They don't even pay me for this job, and now I've got an extra assignment to do outside working hours. 'Write a short article on global warming,' she said. Really?" Toni reached out for a napkin and wiped his fingers while shaking his head. "What are we, in school? 'An original angle to look at it from.' Original? What's original today?" He threw his hands in the air.

Global warming, he typed and stopped.

He hated his trainee job, he hated writing, and he hated Aalborg.

Well, OK, he didn't hate Aalborg, although it was the last big (well, relatively big) city in this tiny Northern country. There were fun people here, and there was always something happening, an Avant-garde art exhibition with an after-party in one corner, a film workshop in the second, pubs, board-game cafes in the third. And so many free events. Some even had free welcome drinks. The only problem was the cold and the dark. Even above zero, for him, felt like minus ten.

But that would be half the problem, if he could go to those fun corners, where smaller and larger crowds collected. Yet, here he was sitting in his apartment the size of a shoe-box and writing an article on global warming.

Toni leaned back in his chair, letting his hands fall onto his lap. He wasn't writing the article. He had to admit that he was just sitting there, looking at the screen with only two words at the top of the document, "Global warming."

The simple fact was, he didn't want to write it. He had always hated writing. Designing, yes. That was his thing. Give him anything graphic. But writing! Words were for speaking and throwing into the air. But putting them down on paper or screen?!

His boss, however, had asked him to write the article. She said, "Write it for your sake. Express your thoughts and feelings on the topic without being in a hurry. You must have an opinion about it."

Well, first of all, he was Italian. Being in a hurry, especially when speaking, was in his DNA. And second, what did he care about global warming? He couldn't change anything about it, could he?

But even if he wasn't paid for this job, he wanted to keep it, because Toni knew he could get a paid job after that.

Choose The News (CTN ApS) was a young and agile startup, who created an app with the same title. The idea was to offer a tool to users where they could choose the news they wanted to read depending not only on their interests but also on their mood. That feature appealed to many. You could select among delicately formulated categories, such as "need uplifting," "feisty," "seeking where I can help," and many others.

There was also a weekly printed news magazine, which was structured like those "Choose Your Own Adventure" books, where the readers could navigate through the various pages of the Manga-book-sized booklet. The end of every article estimated the readers' mood. It gave the readers a choice, depending on whether they needed something to uplift their mood or deepen the topic.

The app and the magazine were a hit in Denmark, and the printed format of Choose The News was quickly subsidized, enabling more copies to be printed after quickly selling out. The English branch was sky-rocketing, and several British and American authors moved to Aalborg (of all places!) to be part of the staff. Toni was lucky to have gotten the trainee job. More than one hundred other people were trying to get it, and Toni knew that with his rate of lost jobs and rejections in the five years since finishing his master's program at the university in Aalborg, getting this job was a miracle.

There was also the prospect of becoming the manager of the Italian branch. He was the only Italian at CTN so far, and Laura wanted to open offices in the countries her employees came from. The idea was that the branch managers took care of the local teams from Aalborg as a home base but could travel to their native countries within the scope of their work, while having a well-paid job in Denmark. And they were allowed to open the branch in their home-towns or nearby if they could find a good team there.

Well, Laura hadn't explicitly said she wanted to open a branch in Italy. Nor that she had Toni in mind for the task. He wasn't employed by Choose The News yet. But he was almost an employee, right? In training, but he worked there, damn it!

To manage the branch in Italy from Aalborg would be a dream job for him. And if he were honest, it was already a dream job for him now, as it was. Each day a new task, fresh colors, unique designs. And everything had to be fast. Both for the daily digital issue for the app and for the weekly Manga-magazine, as Toni thought of the little booklet, which he had to admit he himself loved.

But it seemed he wasn't a dream employee for Laura. She was almost always frowning when she considered his work and often suggested amendments and corrections.

Laura was a petite young woman, looking like one of those Manga characters herself. Big brown eyes, long brown hair gathered in a high-bound ponytail. She did the same studies as Toni, two years his junior. She moved to Aalborg from Copenhagen after attending Danish courses, and shortly after Lily's death.

Toni shook his head. It was a long time since he'd thought of Lily. Why should he anyway? She was just one of his peers at the university, and he had many. But she was the only one who had died just before finishing their master's program. Yeah, somehow, her death affected everyone in his year—Toni included.

Lily was his rival, and they always competed for the score and who would get the higher grade.

Toni loved competing for the grade, and winning in any card, board, or computer game he touched. Being smaller than the other boys in his class and neighborhood was hard, and he got beaten up quite often. So, he made sure he would be the fastest to run, and the best when there were tournaments for almost any game, especially board and computer games. That is why he learned the rules and every possible winning tactic to any game he could put his hands on and made sure he won as often as he could.

The winning was important to Toni. It helped him to build a reputation in his neighborhood as the most successful gamer. With that, he gained some trepidation and respect, and the beating from the bullies reduced. The bullies, not having the coolness factor afforded by winning games, only enjoyed respect (or rather fear) for short periods. So, Toni, as the best gamer around, started receiving their protection instead. But he made sure, and he had his mother to thank for reminding him, not to forget where he started. He was careful not to become a bully himself, and even taught those he beat in games a few tricks on how to win.

Lily was different from all his opponents. She had tremendous fun challenging him and making jokes. She had no respect for his skills in gaming, and she made a game out of everything, including gaming. Winning wasn't as serious for her as for Toni, but it seemed to be so effortless for her.

Winning against Lily in grades or games (they used to play with her boyfriend Will and Miriam, who was Lily's best friend and with whom Lily shared an apartment close to the city center, as well as their study-buddies for hours) became fun.

After her death, the winning for him and being the best in his year became easy and effortless, but boring. He no longer felt challenged, and all the color was gone.

He was still one of the best when he graduated. But writing his master's thesis was torture, and the feedback he got from his supervisor said everything: *Technically — outstanding, creatively — lacking*. But they still let him graduate.

And this morning, Laura repeated his supervisor's words, "You are a technically brilliant graphic designer. There is no tool you don't know or means you haven't tried. You are excellent. But what we need here is a soul, burning for our idea, with curiosity, passion. You don't seem like you have fun here. But fun and passion are what we need here in the long run."

Toni expected her to fire him on the spot, so desperate was her look when she told him that. But then she said, "OK, another try. I've learned that writing something down can clear the mind and heart, and be very therapeutic. Let's take the topic that is all over the news and that everyone has an opinion on."

And then she told him her idea was global warming. She said Toni had to have something the next day. After his shocked reaction, she ran her hands over her face, exhaled, and said, "Toni, we are a quick business. News doesn't wait. And you know that if you give people two days for a task they will take that long and complain it wasn't long enough, even if they could do it in five minutes. Do you have an appointment tonight?"

He had to admit that he didn't.

"OK, then. Write, however, short. Three hundred words would be enough. And you don't need to give me a polished version. Whatever comes to your mind. You can even use a timer so that this task doesn't take up too much of your evening. But bring me something tomorrow. And we will see what we can do next."

Yeah, thought Toni now. Next will be that he loses this unpaid job, and his supervisor at the job center will look at him again with that wordless question, "What's wrong with you?"

He needed to write this essay. He looked at the page in front of him. OK. He'd check his e-mails and then set the timer to write this damn article.

∗∗

There were a couple of e-mails in his mailbox. One of them was a notification about the third blog post by gamefulwriting.com.

Toni wasn't sure why he was reading this blog, having thoroughly checked the credibility of the site.

The idea of combining something he hated with games, which he enjoyed but no longer had much time for, seemed in itself ridiculous. Why would anyone want to do it?

Nowadays, he was passionate about graphic design and could research different techniques for hours, trying them all out.

Passion made sense. "Gameful Writing" sounded like someone trying to force fun onto something tedious. Toni glanced at his unfinished pizza and smirked. This Gameful Writing idea was like trying to turn a pizza into a French dish by adding Herbs de Provence.

Maybe he should write that down. But no. Laura wanted him to write about global warming.

OK, it wouldn't hurt to read this little blog. Who knew what could come of it.

Welcome back to the Gameful Writing blog. It is blog post three or Level Three of your writing game. Today we will talk about how to turn the third type of writing, of the five I outlined in my first blog post (click here), into fun games. And this third type is about pieces we have committed to but which we either don't want to write, or consider unnecessary. We've all had those bits of writing. Just think of all those exams and graduation papers!

"Now, you're talking!" Toni said out loud, and leaned back with satisfaction. The first two blog posts were amusing and something had compelled him to read them. In fact, he only meant to skim through them but found himself going back and re-reading them in full.

But this one promised to be what he needed. He was skeptical that it would do any good, but at least it directly addressed his particular challenge. "OK, surprise me," he said to his laptop, straightened his back, and continued to read.

If you hate to do the writing that has been asked of you, or any task for that matter, you probably resent other aspects of your life as well.

Toni grunted, "You bet I do."

You wouldn't be the first, nor the last, in this situation, although you might feel like nobody could match the depths of your misery. And if you try to convince someone of your misery, they will only try to illustrate their suffering and probably try to prove that they are more miserable. We, humans, are competitive this way. If there's nothing else to compete about, then we will compete about misery.

Trust me, I did that too and sometimes even today I catch myself trying to. How shall I put it? Well, I have some issues with my health.

Ah, screw it! I have cancer, and the doctors can't agree on how long I have left to live. When you get such a diagnosis, it strikes you full in the stomach, even if the cancer is growing somewhere else. It is for me.

What I see now but didn't see when my family, friends, and I found out that I had cancer, is that we all competed to show how sad and miserable we were about it. Only when I turned the figurative "spotlight" away from myself and from how I thought I felt, and just listened to my loved ones, only then did I see that they were scared of what it would be like to lose me.

I am not losing anyone. On the contrary, I've got more support and love than ever. From people I knew from my childhood, those I met throughout my life and now complemented with several doctors and plentiful nurses. But they don't have this richness of help. Wittingly and unwittingly, I have become an integral part of their lives, and now for them there is a real danger of losing that part.

I am getting a ton of painkillers to make my time as comfortable as chemo, and other such things can be (which they are not; they suck, to be honest; sorry I can't find a better word to describe what I feel about chemo). But those around me don't get any painkillers for their heartache.

Yes, you guessed right. I started this project for those dear to me. But maybe not quite or not only as you think. It is not only to help them to go through this. But it is also for me to learn how to experience fully and without grudge what is asked of me, including that damn chemo. (Well, I do sometimes swear when I play games, so don't judge me for swearing about the chemotherapy.)

So yes, you guessed right again, I give myself points and badges for each chemo session, and for each time I take my medicine. You are the first to learn about me doing it, and my loved ones will know it when they find out that I wrote this, but for now, this is your and my secret. And I love secrets. As long as they are kind, empowering, uplifting, and fun to find out, remember?

There is something else I found out about chemo and all those meds with side effects that I have to take. I realized that even if I thought I hated getting the shots and taking the meds, I had to admit that taking them was a part of the bigger dream. The dream is to prolong my time on earth as much as possible, so that I can spend it with my family and friends and gather a few more moments with them. So, for now, my part of the game is to take all the power-ups I need to gain more life power. I can't believe how direct the analogy is between video games and my situation!

You might wonder what that has to do with your hated work or the thesis you have to write. Well, I have news for you. If you haven't ripped the page (even if only figuratively) with the assignment into small pieces and thrown it into your supervisor's or boss's face, then you also want to write it.

There is some part of you that sees the truth about the assignment, that there is value in it, for you and others. And you hate yourself for seeing it.

You don't have to hate yourself anymore. You are not alone in beating yourself up. We all do this, at least once in a while. Let's do a test. Refresh your browser page and see if anyone wrote "I am" to the following question. "Are you ever hard on yourself and think that you or what you do is not good enough?" Feel free to answer it yourself, but you don't have to. Just refresh and see what happens.

Toni scrolled down and discovered there were three "I am" answers before the other two "I am" answers mixed with reports on earning both reading and writing badges. He refreshed and saw how the side marker on his browser moved from the bottom to the half of the page. He scrolled down and discovered tens of "I am" and reports and words of gratitude.

Toni drew a couple of deep breaths. He scrolled back up to where he stopped reading, framed his face with his hands, and continued reading.

Shocking, right? I love those commercials that put people in the position of seeing how hard they are on themselves. And it's tempting to judge ourselves for judging ourselves, however ridiculous that sounds when you write and read it. Judging for judging for judging for complaining about complaining and about judging again.

So where do we go from here? Well, let's see what we do when we get stuck in games? We see where we are (for example, in a hole we fell into in a video game), then we double-check where the finish line is, or the "win-state" as game designers call it. Then we jump or crawl out of the hole and proceed one step at a time, double-checking all the time where the win-state is and continuing to make steps and beneficial detours (like gathering power-ups), but in the end bringing us to the win-state.

You can do the same with the writing piece you think you hate, but which we've established deep inside you need and want to do because, in truth, it is the power-up that will boost you toward the win-state, which you want beyond many other things, if not everything.

Toni sighed. "OK, OK, I see that now. You got me here. But how do I write the damn thing? I still haven't got a clue."

If you still resist putting your timer on for five minutes or even thirty seconds and just writing, then I am here to help.

Do you know how game designers get people to play their games? By introducing ridiculous rules. Often the more ridiculous the rules are, the more people play those games.

I bet you know more than one person who plays either badminton, hockey, tennis, ping-pong, baseball, cricket, or golf. And yet, in all these games, none of the players who want to win the game would do the straightforward and most logical thing, which is to go and grab that little object they all hunt for or throw around, and put it in the goal net, small hole, or onto the opponent's field. Instead, every one of them willingly and dutifully takes a hockey stick, a bat, a club, or a racket and hits or hunts for that little, tiny object with all their might and skill. They do all that to win that match of their favorite game, regardless of how small or big the prize might be.

So, if you want to win this round of the writing game, then here's the ridiculous rule for you.

Get all the gadgets, take all of them under your desk or table, and write.

"What?" Toni took his hands away from his face and put them between himself and his computer on the desk. He leaned a bit closer to make sure he'd read it right.

Yes, you read that right. I suggest, no, in fact, I insist that you write under your desk or table. Otherwise, no writing badge for you today.

"Seriously? You got to be kidding me!"

Yes, I am serious. The only variant I will allow here is if you choose to write in a place that is as or even more ridiculous than sitting under a table. Like sitting in the kitchen sink, for example.

Toni grunted. "No, thank you. Under the table is ridiculous enough."

He went and checked that his apartment door was locked, which he rarely did. He couldn't believe what he was about to do, but he wanted to make sure that no one caught him actually doing this stupid challenge.

"What was your gadget list again?" He clicked back to the first blog post and got his computer, his mobile with the timer app open, and a cup of espresso along with a glass of water, which he set a little outside. He didn't want to risk a flood on his floor or, heaven forbid, his computer. Then he would be completely screwed tomorrow.

Toni tried to make himself comfortable, but it was so damn hard sitting on the floor. Why did the Danes love wood for their floors? He had no idea. Since, as this damn blogger had helpfully pointed out, judging and complaining didn't help, Toni put his laptop aside, got the blanket from his sofa, folded it, spread it under his desk, and sat on it. Better. Not much, but better.

I've got another helpful tip for you.

"You call making people write their graduate papers under the table helpful? If you expect me to do anything else like this, then I am out of here, I'm telling you!" He hoped that the blogger could feel his outrage.

Before you start the timer, go on and write the following sentence, "I write this while sitting under my desk (in the kitchen sink, or under the kitchen, dinner, hopefully not a coffee table — you'd need to lie down under it, and that would slow your writing speed ;D)."

So, did you write that down?

"OK, OK, I can do that." Toni typed:

I write this while sitting under my desk. I have no idea why I'm doing that, and please don't ask me the details, but here I am sitting under my desk and writing an article on global warming.

Toni stopped himself. "Whoa! What was that?! I forgot to start the timer." He narrowed his eyes, leaned forward, and looked around his room. Everything looked the same as always, or slightly different from the perspective of being under his desk. He shook his head and briefly checked the end of the third blog post, which he recalled he'd not yet finished reading. He saw that there were just wishes of fun ("Yeah, really? Well, OK.") and the usual countdown, "Ready, set, go!", which looked ridiculous being on a screen, as opposed to shouted out by someone at a kids sporting event. Now under his desk, Toni had no words for the stupidity of all this.

With another grunt of disdain, he set the timer to thirty minutes ("five minutes are for sissies") and went back to the paragraph he just wrote.

***

My boss asked me for my opinion on global warming. Do you want to know it too? No? Well, I'll tell you anyway because I want to get done with this assignment.

I think global warming sucks.

There you have it. That is the bottom line anyway; however you try to formulate it and make it look pretty.

Do you want an illustration or analogy?

I've got one for you.

Get your behind under a desk or a table, exactly like me now. Feel free to take everything you love, people, pets, and things, with you. Make sure you all have space to sit. Get more tables if you need them. Then ask a friend whom you might love a little less than those with you under the table to take a large sheet of plastic and seal it with tape on the floor all around the tables you are sitting under.

You should be intelligent enough to realize that if you don't tear a big enough hole into the plastic, you will suffocate at some point and die. You and all who are stupid enough to join you under the table.

Boy, am I glad that I don't own even the tiniest of tablecloths, plastic or otherwise.

Now, on Earth, we are not sealed with a plastic sheet we can break through to get air to breathe.

The atmosphere separates the space we live in from the universal vacuum beyond, in which there's no (or negligibly little) oxygen, which we need to survive. The ozone hole to the universal void might not be getting bigger anymore, thanks to the reduction in use of ozone-depleting chemicals undertaken in the 1990s. Still, I read that the hole might also be reducing in size because of increasing temperatures on earth. There you have it — that global warming.

What shall we do then, and what did we do so far as human beings who have the power to create and innovate? We have happened to take under our figurative table, not only what we treasure. We had enough stupidity to take huge ovens and waste generators into this little space under the table.

Isn't it enough that we fart and poop ourselves? C'mon! Let's bring a little sensitivity here.

Some politicians talk about environmental awareness of the masses, or rather they address each one of us, trying to micro-manage the consumption and waste from a distance.

Well, you, idiots, you are part of this mass. You are human too!

You talk about people using less plastic and recycling. Well then, do that yourself, be the example. But beyond that, close the factories producing all that new plastic, and polluting the air, or at least stop supporting and paying them. Make them reuse what they got, not create more garbage. Make them do everything to make the air we all breathe cleaner. You've got the power given to you by people, by us. What are you waiting for? Why don't you use it as those who gave it to you hoped you would? Are you waiting for the first person to suffocate?

Remember that sooner or later, you'll also suffocate. You are under this table too!

The next morning, Toni edited his piece briefly. He shook his head most of the time he was editing the rant. That is the only way he could think of it. Where did all that emotion come from? He was usually in control and was proud that even if he was Italian, he could keep his cool. But he didn't have time now to write another piece. This rant was all he had. And he quietly admitted that he had fun writing it. He wasn't sure what it was, but there was something in this rant of his that he liked. He even admitted to having fun writing it, in the comment he added claiming his materially non-existent Gameful Writing Badge. There was no way he was drawing this thing. But it was fun to claim it in the comments and have people congratulate him. "Congrats, Comment 75!" "Well done!" and "Way to go!" Toni had rarely heard those words before, even including the wins he gained when he played games as a child, and he had to admit that getting them did feel good. He only wished Laura could have seen it, then she might have changed her opinion about his attitude.

He scanned through his piece one more time and sent it to Laura half an hour before she came to work.

Toni didn't approach Laura to let her know he'd sent the assignment. He hurriedly pretended to work as soon as he saw her starting her computer up, and probably checking her e-mails. Was his e-mail the first one she would read?

He tried to work on the design for a new segment, both for their app and the mini-magazine. The full employee from the UK and the manager of the British team, Steve, had asked him for it two days ago. But Toni couldn't do more than a few clicks. He had to check on what Laura was doing. He glanced through the glass walls of her office over and over again.

Laura glanced once at Toni, and he hurried to look at his screen. So she was reading his article.

After a few minutes of reading, Laura clasped her mouth with her right hand.

Uh-oh.

Then her shoulders started shaking. And then she wiped away a tear.

What? Was Laura crying over his article? What was he supposed to do now?

In the next moment, Laura turned to face him and waved for him to come over to her.

To his shame, Toni only now realized that his nose wasn't pointing at his screen but hanging way out over his laptop. He'd been caught spying on his boss while she read the piece he wrote.

Swallowing hard, he half-nodded. That's all he could manage. Then he stood up and went to face the music.

Laura gestured to him to sit, still wiping, no, dabbing with a tissue at her perfectly styled eyes.

Toni closed the glass door behind him. There was no need for his colleagues to hear how she fired him, the trainee.

Laura looked at him, and Toni realized that she was smiling. "Toni, I hoped writing this piece, or any piece, would open you up, but I didn't expect this." She gestured at the screen displaying his miserable scribble.

Toni cringed. "Laura, I'm sorry, this is just not my —"

"I love it!" Laura's smile widened into a full one.

"What?"

"I love it. It's brilliant. Would it be OK with you if we included it in next week's booklet and our own segment in the app?"

Toni opened and closed his mouth. He stared for a couple of seconds, then forced himself to say something. "You want to use it? But wait. It's not uplifting or motivating or anything like what you try to do. It's a rant."

"It is." Laura continued grinning at him. "And that's why I love it. It's so utterly yours. Open, direct, funny, and loud. But most of all: engaging. That's how you are at our social events. But somehow, you stop yourself from being you in the office. You seem to suppress your passion, trying to act indifferent and cool, maybe. But this suppression shows in your work. This piece reveals what you can really do."

Toni didn't know what to think. He frowned. "My passion got me fired and even kicked in the butt a couple of times. It got me into enough trouble in so many places."

"Maybe those places were wrong for you? Or maybe you haven't shown them your true self as you did with us.

Which is the same thing." Laura's smile disappeared, but the warmth in her eyes remained.

"What are you trying to say?"

"I think you would be the right fit for our company. But most of us have multiple types of tasks and projects. It is not only graphic design, but writing too. And also management. We are going to open branches in various countries, but I would like to have coordination from here. They'll have their managers there too, who'll be doing the writing and design too. So basically, each of us here is the designer, writer, editor, and manager, and I hoped you would be interested in that too."

"But I am!" He almost blurted out, "I hoped you would give me the Italian branch" but managed to keep his mouth shut.

Laura looked at her screen with his article and then back at Toni. "The fact that you took on the challenge and did that shows me that you are interested. Here's what I think." She narrowed her eyes a little then relaxed them again. "I think you'd do great at opening and managing the Italian branch of the CTN."

Toni held his breath. Was he that obvious? There hadn't been concrete talk of opening an Italian branch yet. It was just his fantasy, seeing all these considerations to open new offices. But even if Laura had a typical Italian name and could have been confused for an Italian girl, she wasn't Italian. She was Brazilian, so it would be more straightforward for her to open a branch in her home country first.

"But as I said," Laura said, interrupting Toni's thoughts, "every one of us needs to be a writer too, and first and foremost creative and resourceful. Not being afraid to blurt out even the most ludicrous of ideas. Would you be interested in writing this kind of rant, as well as researching and finding some funny and enlightening rants and tirades online and in print?"

"Are you talking about a new segment? A ranting one? Like 'A rant a day to keep stupor at bay'?"

Laura laughed. "I like that. We could also call it 'Ranty.'" Laura chuckled as Toni grimaced. Then she nodded. "Yes, I am talking about a new segment of honest, direct, and eye-opening as well as funny reportage and opinions expressed on various topics of the day. And which would use the word 'idiot' regularly." Laura grinned.

Toni caught himself smiling.

"So, what do you say? Would you be willing to take over the whole segment, including the research, design, writing, and management of it?"

"Wait, you want me to be the editor of this new ranting segment and do all the work for it as well? Plus, the Italian branch?"

"Yes, but you don't have to be the only contributor. You will collect rants from the rest of the office too, and are welcome to contribute to the more 'peaceful,'" Laura mimicked inverted commas with the index and middle fingers of her hands "columns we have. We are all one team here, and even if we expand, I'd love to remain one close-knit team helping everyone's projects to grow and prosper."

"It sounds like marriage," Toni blurted out and looked shocked at Laura. What had happened to make him start saying his most stupid thoughts out loud in the office? And especially to his boss?!

Laura erupted with laughter, clasped her mouth with both hands, then removed them and started dabbing at her eyes again while trying to stop the giggles.

Toni laughed. "I'm sorry. I don't know what happened last night, but I must admit that your assignment released something that I didn't see. And I love the idea of having so many hats in the company. I do seem to be good at ranting, and not only because of my Roman heritage."

Laura giggled again.

Toni returned the smile and then frowned. "There is one thing though, which I can't promise. I can't promise that I won't lapse into this suppressed mode again and become defensive or cool. I thought cool was good.

You're cool." He could have beaten himself again. Where was his skill for suppression when he needed it?

Laura grinned at him, "That's all right, Toni. We all have our downtimes, and that's what teams are for. To support each other and help out in those times. But no team member would be able to help when the door is locked and barricaded. However, I have a feeling that something happened last night when you wrote the article that hinders you from locking that door. Did you really sit under the table when you wrote it?"

"I did."

"You didn't." Laura's eyes filled with tears again, and she doubled with laughter.

Then she wanted to know who or what managed to get one of the most stubborn and unmovable people to do something that ridiculous and produce something more than she had expected. Before letting him answer she confided that until she read his article it hadn't crossed her mind to have a rant segment. Then she motioned him to follow her to their company's kitchen, get coffee and water for them and tell her all he knew about Gameful Writing.

An hour later, Toni was at his desk jotting down the tasks in his to-do list:

- Write a short feature on Gameful Writing, and share the site and the blog with everyone in the office.

- Write a feature on my experience as a trainee at CTN and how Laura offered me a full-time job.

- Finish the design for Steve's Happy Gardening segment.

- Get Steve to edit my 1st rant and the two features. If he can't do all of them, ask around the office for someone else to help out.

- Suggest three titles for the rant segment and the basic design features.

- Define components for the rant segment: Our rant (written, sometimes maybe podcast; discuss it with Laura), written rant by others (online, social media, ranting books, etc.), video, and radio (podcasts).

- Get Laura's approval.

Deadline for everything: This week.

Toni looked at the list. It was incomplete, and it was huge. How was he going to make it? He had no idea, but he had to grin.

He opened the third blog post of Gameful Writing, scrolled down to the form for a new comment and typed:

I have no idea who you are, and yesterday before reading the third post, I thought that you were stupid and impossible. But your ridiculous challenge to write under the table did something I never expected. It changed me somehow. My day today doesn't feel as miserable as the days before. To be honest, it feels fantastic. And I want to thank you for that. Oh, I almost forgot. I just got the offer of a dream job. That's one of the fantastic bits. :D

Toni pressed "Post" and went back to designing Steve's segment. To his surprise, he now knew exactly how to do it.

Chapter 4: Sofie

*

Sofie loved her work at the university. After the hiatus with breast cancer, she could finally finish writing her thesis.

The thesis was basically written. Sofie just needed to wrap it up. Write the conclusions chapter and update the introduction.

But something was missing. Sofie couldn't pin down what.

No, if she were honest with herself, she knew exactly what it was—the meaning of it all was missing. The purpose, if you like. Why was she writing a thesis about the history of graphic design, starting with the stone age and ending with the first half of the twentieth century? The pre-history of computer design, if you will; all those scribbles and creations in stone, on papyrus, paper, and micro-film? Why was it so important, besides not to forget it?

Well, yes, it was fun. And graphic, or you could say, any type of design was a huge trend nowadays. But why learn the history of it? Why was she doing it? Who cared why it developed the way it did? Wasn't it just about creativity and following what was fun? Didn't everyone have to find out what was fun for them? Could you really teach it?

For a bachelors or even a masters thesis, the question of why wouldn't matter that much. The "how?" could be answered, and it would be enough. But for an assistant professor writing a Ph.D. thesis, it was vital to know why she was doing what she was doing.

Sofie stood up from her desk, grabbed the printed introduction to her thesis, and started walking around her house.

Half an hour later, she returned to her desk, the pages rolled into a tube. Tapping the paper tube against her palm or staring at the pages didn't help. OK, Sofie thought, let's see what's happening in the world for ten minutes and then go back to work on the thesis.

She set the timer to ten minutes. She'd bought two timers (one for their little office, one for the rest of the house) a week after reading the first blog post on gamefulwriting.com. She and her family had used the timers often since then. For example, for making sure that screen time didn't exceed non-screen time for all of them, especially the children. The beeping of the timers removed all discussion of how long any of them had been using their screens.

Now, having started the timer, Sofie looked at her e-mails. There were four of them. One was a newsletter, and three were notifications of new posts from the many blogs she subscribed to. She disregarded the others and clicked the one from the Gameful Writing blog.

She'd been surprised when she got the first notification, and wondered if it was a mistake. Before clicking on the link, she checked the authenticity of the site and then its contents. The many resources on anthropology immediately intrigued her since studying the history of humanity was one of her professional loves. So, in the end, Sofie didn't unsubscribe but instead read all the posts and earned all the badges so far. She shared the approach with her family, and with immense curiosity embarked on an adventure to discover various areas in their lives where they could combine everyday tasks with games.

But the last post made Sofie wish she could meet the person writing it and give him or her a big hug. The blogger opened up about having cancer and having been through it herself, Sofie wanted to reach out and help with encouraging words, as her family and friends did when she went through the experience. Even though the blogger warned that he or she wouldn't be answering the comments, Sofie immediately commented with words of encouragement to the author and looked for a few days afterwards for any hint of an answer. But there wasn't any.

Sofie hoped that the author was still alive and recovering. She hoped dearly that these blog posts weren't scheduled beforehand by someone who already died. Sofie embraced herself and rubbed her arms against the chill she felt, but which she knew wasn't coming from cold.

"OK," she said aloud, trying to pull herself away from the gloomy thoughts, "let's read the post."

**

Welcome back to the Gameful Writing blog.

Only two more types of writing to go. Here is Level Four of your writing game. Writing to explore yourself.

Any type of writing will reveal something new to you about yourself if you just let it.

You might be wondering why you are doing something. But as we've seen in previous posts, anything you do and don't give up at some point, you also want to do or at least try out before giving up.

Any piece of writing you do, however impersonal and dry you think it is, should have your personal touch. If you write it, it is a piece of you. Own it.

Remember that in games it is the same. Each move you make in those is yours, no one else's. And you own it. The same is true of your writing game.

In a minute, I'll ask you to go back to your writing and discover what there is of you in the task you need to accomplish. If you feel like there is nothing, then the solution is even simpler. Bring a part of you in there. If you know what part that is, then go to your work-in-progress and incorporate that part into it.

Are you still here? You are?

That may be because despite agreeing that there is or should be a part of you in whatever you do and there is a very personal reason for why you do what you do, you can't see it clearly. An activity or a project draws you like a magnet, and you seem unable to get rid of it, even given the chance, but you don't understand what is binding you to it.

So, what are you supposed to do? Is anything wrong? Anything missing?

When you feel something is missing or not quite right, then something might be both missing and not. Let me explain.

You and whatever you do, or did until now, is whole and perfect, whatever state or shape you are or it is. But your searching feeling and the need to move forward or dig deeper is perfect too. "Perfect," don't forget, also means "done" and "completed."

So if something doesn't leave you in peace and you feel like you should go on a quest (often just figuratively and in exploring your thought processes and feelings), then there is a reason for it.

First of all, there's the reason of curiosity. We've all been born curious. That is how we grow, in all senses of the word.

How far you go with your curiosity is up to you. Only you can define when something is done, closed, and perfect for you.

For example, if you are a painter standing at an easel and letting spectators observe how you work, you and them would have different opinions on when your painting is finished, at times them being sure that you're done with the art you do for them, long before you think so.

Only you can define whether something is "missing" for you. Take a non-judgmental look at what is telling you that what you do is (or you as a person are) incomplete.

Is it fear of putting your writing (since we talk here about writing, but of course, you can see that it applies to anything) out there, and being judged for it?

If yes, then flip this coin and realize that you are ready and even excited to take your work to the next level, whether it is sending it to your editor, agent, or self-publishing it. Your fear is just an indicator that it's time to press that "Start" button.

Let's reformulate it. Your worry is the excitement you feel before playing that new game, the game of sending your manuscript to the editor, submitting your thesis, or publishing your work.

But if after becoming equipped with the awareness above, you still feel that something is missing, then trust yourself and search for this bit.

I learned that when I feel that something is missing, then that missing part is me.

That's why, all of a sudden, in the last post, I told you about my cancer and how I try to deal with it. My challenges are a part of my journey, a part of me. So why not share them with you? Otherwise, my blog would be just a disembodied rambling about games and writing.

The same is true of your writing. Whatever you do and whoever assigned it to you, and however challenging it might appear to you, there is a bit of you in it, especially if it has gone on a long time already.

If discovering yourself and looking at your feelings seems hard to you, even if I keep telling you "Look at them non-judgmentally," you might still have thoughts like "Easy for you to say!" and "What the hell is non-judgmental anyway?!", then I have a game for you to play.

I will send you on a quest to find the mission of your writing game. So your work-in-progress is already a game. We've established that. You might know the win-state of your game, that is what you get when you finish the project (a degree, a published book to your name, etc.). But what is the mission of it? Are you saving someone in this game, like a princess? Are you solving a puzzle, like in an Escape Room? Some games don't explain any rules but throw you immediately into action and let you discover the rules by finding clues.

Here, you have this kind of quest.

So, study yourself for five, more, or fewer minutes. You could use those variants with dice or cards to determine for how long.

You could also go for a walk. Or you could wash the dishes like Agatha Christie was famous for doing, where she claimed to get her best ideas.

Thus, do whatever appears helpful for you to find the mission of your writing game. Again, it is there.

Don't dismiss any of the thoughts or ideas that come. Your gut is your compass. Others would call this "instrument" heart or intuition. Whatever it is for you, listen to it. Anything it points to is a resource.

See where you are, what you feel, what moved you to be where you are, what are the goals and dreams towards which you want to proceed, what are you doing now, and where does this step lead you in relation to your goals and dreams.

Sorry for repeating things, but I feel like I have to. Find your mission and trust that there is one. Just observe what you are doing and where your gut (heart or intuition) sends you, and move along. Don't be afraid to get lost somewhere. Your trusty timer is there to bring you back.

How I see the mission of this game for you, you might ask? I am convinced that you will discover something that you don't know yet, but something you very much want to know. That's the magic of being here, moving in small steps, and treating everything like the best and most exciting game in the world.

Now, all that's left is to send you on your quest.

Ready, set, go!

***

After reading the blog post, Sofie re-set the timer, which went off in the middle of reading the post, for one hour, pressed "Start," exhaled deeply and looked through the copies of photographs in the thick folder for her thesis. Somehow her thoughts turned to her family, her grandparents, her big sister, her parents, her children, and her husband. Her first thought was to dismiss them as distractions from her purpose of finishing the introduction and conclusions to her Ph.D. thesis, but then she recalled the advice in the blog post she just read.

The blogger said, *"Don't dismiss any of the thoughts or ideas that come. Your gut is your compass. Anything it points to is a resource."*

Surely, her family was a big part of her.

"OK, Sofie," she said quietly to herself, "let's find out." She stood up, took her coffee cup to the kitchen, and smiled gratefully at the memory of her husband suggesting he take their children to visit his parents so that she could finish writing her thesis. A pang of guilt rose, but again she thought, what's the reason for me thinking of it? She recalled the message her husband had written with the suggestion. He had used several emojis.

She stopped. Why did she think of her family members when she had been working with hieroglyphs and other pre-historic graphic objects? Yes, everyone agreed that the size of the symbols on those old stones and papyrus meant something. Some said that it was because the size communicated the power of the winning side. Some lines were interpreted as early attempts at graphic design. But why did she think of her family almost immediately? What was the connection between the family and those pre-historic documents?

She stopped in the middle of washing her cup. She felt an impulse. It felt like she was moments from discovering treasure. Like standing on the spot marked with a cross on a treasure map. She just needed to dig. She finished washing the cup, put it on the drip tray, dried her hands with the towel, and walked into the master bedroom. She lifted her part of the king-size bed she and her husband bought when they moved in together, and took out a big box. Then she took out a folder in a plastic bag. This folder had both copies and originals of various documents from her side of the family. Especially letters. Her love for history prompted many relatives to send her all kinds of materials that they knew she would preserve and take good care of.

She took the folder out of its plastic wrapping and brought it into their little office. She put it on the floor, sat beside it, and took out a bunch of letters, spreading them — each in a separate plastic wrapping — on the floor in front of her.

She looked at them, taking one at a time, and found that there was something that connected them all. She looked closer and found herself selecting three letters. She put them on top of the other letters in front of her.

The first two were letters her grandparents sent to each other during World War II. Theirs was an unlikely marriage of a German soldier and a young woman fighting on the side of the French Resistance. Sofie was named after her grandmother.

Sofie junior grew up in Germany, close to Hamburg, with her sister and her parents. She often visited her grandparents, who lived in a village nearby. Her grandmother Sofie loved to say that she wanted to live in Germany after the war to contribute at least a little bit in avoiding anything like Hitler happening there again. Grandmother Sofie loved to be asked during family gatherings what her biggest contribution to world peace was. She always answered the same way, by gesturing with pride at the big family in front of her.

Sofie, herself, met her husband Keld in Germany while studying in Hamburg. She never managed to live far away from her parents and grandparents until she married Keld and moved with him to Aalborg, where he came from. Sofie's parents and older sister still lived in the Hamburg area, which she treasured because it was just half a day's drive from them.

It had been more than ten years since her grandparents passed away. But Sofie could still remember them well, especially at the family gatherings on various occasions. Both in wheelchairs, always holding hands when seated at a table. They both lived beyond the age of ninety. Mamie Sofie (as all in the family called Sofie's grandmother using the French word for "Grannie") and

Opa Erhard (as Mamie Sofie insisted that her husband be called by his grandchildren with the German word for "Grandpa"; roots were important for her on both sides) lived until ninety-three and ninety-one, respectively. Mamie Sofie loved the fact that she was older. Mamie Sofie used to say that then they had a chance to die close in time to each other. And she happened to be right. Mamie Sofie died first, and Opa Erhard nine months later. He loved saying in the months before his death that his sweetheart was preparing a beautiful little house in heaven for his arrival.

Their love was legendary in the family and beyond. Erhard studied French linguistics before the war and was in love with the language. When the war started he tried to avoid being enlisted but at the threat of being shot and his family executed too, he went to serve, but made sure that he didn't shoot anyone, always aiming in front of the target so no one would be hurt. Sometimes the shootings were in the dark, and the uncertainty of whether Erhard ever injured or even killed someone, tortured him the rest of his life. Erhard met Sofie when his troop occupied Marseilles. She was working in a restaurant frequented by the officers from his unit. He was often taken to interpret. Sofie pretended to know little German, although she was fluent, through her grandparents, who were German aristocrats. Sofie and Erhard fell in love, and Sofie confided in Erhard that she was not only fluent in German but also fighting with the Resistance, getting them all the information she could about the German troops. Erhard confided in Sofie how much he hated the war and Hitler.

Erhard wanted to run away with Sofie and fight with her on the side of the Resistance. But Sofie convinced him that it would be dangerous, not just for them and their relationship, but also endangering the efforts of the Resistance group fighting in Marseilles. So, they had to part ways.

 They exchanged only a handful of letters during the war. Erhard wrote to Sofie in French, and she wrote in German so that if anyone found the letters, they would assume they were from relatives or loved ones in their home countries. Only one person knew of their relationship. It was Sofie's brother Jean. He disapproved of the relationship, but he agreed to smuggle the letters in person between France and Germany, so they couldn't be traced back. Unfortunately, he was killed on one of his missions for the Resistance. Sophie smuggled the last letter she wrote to Erhard during the war herself, handing it to him under the pretence of working for the "feldpost," the German military mail service. They often told the story of having to swallow their emotions upon seeing each other. Erhard always added how lucky they were, that no one from his unit recognized Sofie as the French waitress back in Marseilles. He was relieved when the war ended shortly after, and they no longer had to exchange letters.

Some in the family speculated that Erhard and Sofie moved to Germany after the war because, as a soldier serving in a Nazi army, Erhard might have been condemned in France. Still, the younger Sofie always believed what her grandmother said about wanting to save Germany from another such fate.

Sofie now picked up the two letters, one in German and one in French, that her grandparents had sent to each other. The words were as neutral as they could be, but still formulated in such a way that the recipient could feel the tenderness of the author, "I hope you are safe," "Thinking of you." Sofie's grandparents had developed a unique collection of graphic elements, such as lines of different length, thickness, and shape, to communicate meaning beyond their words. But they also avoided any intricate signs that could be misinterpreted as code. They limited themselves to underlining some words and writing others twice for emphasis.

The third letter she had selected was from her big sister, when Sofie went through chemotherapy. Natalie lived in Germany but often came to visit and stay during that time. She also sent e-mails, text messages, and she often called. That was also the time when Natalie brought Sofie a little package with the letters that their grandparents wrote to each other during the war. Inspired by their example, as she claimed, Natalie wrote letters to Sofie all written in three languages: French, German, and English. French and German had been spoken in their families interchangeably, and all children and grandchildren of grandparents Sofie and Erhard had gotten names of either French or German origin.

Natalie's and Sofie's parents chose French for their girls' names. They said that if they ever had a son, he would have a German name, just like Opa (Grandpa) Erhard. Natalie used to write to Sofie in English too because it was Sofie's favorite. Sofie, in turn, wrote to Natalie interchangeably in French, German, and Italian (Natalie's preferred language). Learning languages in their grandparents' family was like playing music in others. It all started with Opa Erhard's love for the French language and her grandparents' love for each other.

Natalie's letter about Sofie's cancer was special. Frank, open, loving, and hopeful. She said she couldn't even imagine how Sofie must have felt to be diagnosed with cancer shortly after losing one of her students to leukemia.

Wait! Sofie stopped her thoughts. What did I just think about Natalie's letter? She repeated the words out loud, "Frank, open, loving, and hopeful."

Hopeful!

Sofie looked at her grandmother's letter to her grandfather Erhard in German, "Ich hoffe, es geht Dir gut." "I hope you are well." Mamie Sofie wrote the word "hoffe," "hope," three times over.

Hope!

Opa Erhard's letter in French said at the end, "J'espère que la guerre sera bientôt terminée." "I hope the war is over soon." He wrote the sentence in block letters.

J'espère! I hope!

Sofie jumped to her feet and took the folder with her thesis research, containing photographs of pictures of animals in battle, and put it on the floor.

Many historians argued about why some animals, such as goats and geese, were drawn bigger than the bulls and elephants on the enemy's side. There were many theories about why that might be.

But what if the reason was hope? Sofie glanced at Natalie's letter and saw that her sister had underlined the word hope in her letter.

Sofie recalled something and stormed out of their little home office and into the kitchen. There she unclipped a small card from the refrigerator. Her husband and children made it for her before driving away. All three had participated in writing the sweetest of messages, "We hope you have a fun, successful, and productive weekend, full of joy and creativity. Happy writing and finishing!" Sofie looked at the word "hope." It was framed in a floral wreath, which her daughters had drawn for her. Just this word. The word "fun" was emphasized too, and to her amusement, Sofie noticed that the word "productive" had the least emphasis, written in the smallest letters on the card. But the word that got most embellishment was "hope."

Oh, wow!

Sofie took the card with her to her office. She made room on her desk for both folders and spread the three letters and the card on them, leaving the photograph with ancient pictures of domesticated animals visible.

So, it might have been hope the whole time. Throughout the centuries. So what Sofie was teaching through a history of graphic design was, in fact, how to subtly communicate a message of hope, in addition to that captured in words.

Of course, some might argue that hope wasn't the reason for goats and geese to be portrayed bigger than elephants. And many might agree with them. Perhaps, contrary to general understanding, their ancestors had mastered the skills of perspective by that time, and the elephants were portrayed as standing far away. But maybe, just maybe it was a message of hope, saying, "We might have little left after the battle, but we are grateful for what we have, and hope things will be all right in the end."

Whatever those ancestors meant, Sofie knew now what her mission was. She was on a mission to show how hope was demonstrated through graphic design over the centuries. It would require her to re-write some of the chapters, and she probably wouldn't manage to finish it before her family came back, but she could still use most of the material she had produced so far.

The timer went off. Really? Only one hour had passed since she went on this quest? Amazing.

She switched to the browser window, which still displayed the fourth Gameful Writing Blog post and commented:

I earned both the reading and writing badge today and found my mission. It's all about Hope. It always has been. Thank You!

Then she opened the folder with her thesis and happily started her quest of reworking it.

Chapter 5: Torben

*

Torben didn't gain any of the writing badges announced by the Gameful Writing blog. He received all four of the reading badges, and each of them multiple times. But he didn't write as prompted. Nor did he comment on any of them.

He wasn't sure why he got the notification for this blog in the first place. But he knew precisely why he read each of the posts many times and kept all four notifications in his mailbox.

You sound so much like Lily! This thought rotated in his mind many times during the day after he read the third blog post, in which the blogger confided that he or she had cancer.

I wish you were Lily! That would mean you were still alive.

I hope you have better luck than Lily! I wish she had a better chance in life.

And I hope your parents can find the strength to help and support you. I couldn't.

He couldn't banish the shame of his behavior, even five years later.

When others tried to be strong, the two men in Lily's life had fallen apart. Her father was having temper tantrums while her boyfriend drank himself into oblivion. The supposedly strongest people became not only the weakest but also the most unhelpful.

But I wanted to help and wasn't allowed to! This five-year-old stubborn thought popped up again like a defensive shield.

Torben put his mobile down on the kitchen counter and reached for a cup on the shelves above the sink. "For the best father in the world," it said. He remembered how eight-year-old Lily stood proudly announcing that she bought it from her pocket money for Torben's birthday as he was unpacking it.

It was time for him to leave this apartment and go back to Odense. He and Karina could sell it. Or rent it. They bought it shortly after Lily was diagnosed with leukemia. Lily didn't want to move back to Odense or go to Copenhagen to be treated. She wanted to stay in Aalborg and continue her studies in graphic design. Lily was about to start the research for her masters thesis, and she had a supervisor already, when she was diagnosed with cancer. Only ten months later, she was gone. And six of these she spent in a tiring stay in bed interchangeably at home, the little apartment she shared with Miriam, and at the hospital. She was so weak most of that time.

Torben didn't know what still held him in Aalborg. He could do his work from almost anywhere, and hiding in Aalborg from friends and neighbors was convenient. He was wondering if he was hiding from Karina too. She had to be in Odense since she worked at the municipality there and couldn't do her job remotely as he did.

But he couldn't push it further any longer. Karina was the most patient person he knew, and she loved him. But she'd raised the question of whether or not he loved her and wanted to stay with her more than once, and although he always insisted that he did, Torben could see that her faith in the truth of his answer was fading.

Torben tore off a large piece of paper towel, wrapped the cup from Lily in it and put it in the box that had been out for a week already, waiting for him to start packing.

He was about to reach for another cup when a beep on his mobile stopped him. He thankfully took his mobile and hurried out of the kitchen, to delay the packing and returning to Odense for a little bit longer.

**

Welcome back to the Gameful Writing blog. It is the last level in your writing game, Level Five.

I'm glad you made it this far. Can you imagine, it's been four months since the first post and it's now the beautiful month of May. There is no better month to talk about our fifth type of writing than the month preceding the favorite season of most people or most students. :D

The fifth type of writing, as I took the freedom to define it in the first post of the Gameful Writing blog (click here), is writing as a gift.

You might consider it strange that I devoted a whole type of writing to writing cards, notes, and letters to friends and family. However, if you think that it is only about writing thank-you-notes, e-mails, and letters, then you misunderstood me.

Writing as a gift is anything that is meant to be seen by others, or even for yourself to see at a different time. Like writing for the future you.

So, in a way, this type embraces all four previous types. Here is how. You might want it but be afraid of it (Type 1), need to write it like a Sorry note but fret the result (Type 2), resent being told by your partner to write a few words on the card for your in-laws (Type 3), and not know what you need to say to them and why (Type 4). Plus, this type here adds to it. It adds the feeling of a gift for a special occasion, even if there isn't one.

It doesn't just have to be in words. You can draw, you can make a collage, you can type or write text in different colors and shapes. The text can be as simple as "I love you!" or "Thank you for being here for me!", as sophisticated and long as a full-fleshed novel based on true events, or anything in-between.

For whom should you create something like that? For the closest person or people in your life. You can also create it for many, or even the whole world. I had many people in mind (yes, I know that many fantastic people) while creating this site and blog, but I am aware and hope that more would see what I create and start tasting and testing the gameful approach to their writing and life.

Deep down, you know who your first special Do-It-Yourself gift should be for. But you might be afraid to do it.

If you are not afraid and can't wait to start, then proceed to read the next paragraph. But if you do, there is some help at the end of this post.

I suggest that you don't use the timer this time. Approach this more like playing than a game. There are no rules here except your creativity (which is limitless, even if you might not trust me on that). Use any material or words that come your way and put them together like LEGO bricks and create something new and unique. Set the alarm for the next mealtime, but until then, JUST PLAY!

Here is a caveat (a deviation, but not entirely) to what I just said. If you are fascinated by the magic of your timer, then set it up for whatever time you want and when it goes off, record your point, put it on again (as you did in Level Two of the writing game, click here), and continue to play. There are no limits here. You have the freedom, because, yes, you recalled it correctly, you are the co-designer of this game, or play.

When you finish your creation, wrap it up (whatever the format you chose. The above would also apply to an e-mail, a little figuratively, but not completely. Remember that e-mails also contain all sorts of colors and tools to include images and styles to make them creative too).

If you still don't know where to start, then you might never have created a gift to yourself, or you have never considered whatever you do for yourself as a gift. Not even a cup of your beloved espresso macchiato or tea.

If this is the case, then I have an additional quest for you. But first, let me tell you a true story. I read it once in a literary magazine, and I will try to summarize it quickly for you.

A girl was separated from her older sister for three years. There were no mobiles in those times, and they were on two different continents during those three years, seeing each other only during the summer vacations. The mother suggested that the younger daughter wish her older sister "good night" every day in her thoughts when she went to bed. The girl's mother claimed that she would feel closer to her big sister that way.

After those three years, the girls reunited, but their father died shortly after. Now the little girl said "good night" to her father.

Then the girl grew up, got married, and had her own family. She started traveling in connection with her job. The tradition of wishing "good night" to her loved ones in her thoughts, both to the living and those who passed away, remained present throughout her life.

One night, when she was the last to go to bed and her family was already sleeping, the girl, now a woman, wished her loved ones "good night" in her thoughts, and before she closed her eyes to fall asleep, realized something. I never wished "good night" to myself, she thought. But don't I tell my children as often as I can that kindness to others starts with kindness to ourselves?!

So she closed her eyes and said quietly to herself, "Good night, sweetie!" She felt a wave of warmth streaming through her.

More magic happened the next day when she woke up feeling more rested than ever before. The memory of the wave of warmth the moment before she fell asleep accompanied her through the day and came vividly back when her children wrapped her arms around her neck and her husband kissed her. And in those moments, she knew exactly how she could bring joy to her loved ones.

I hope you enjoyed the story. I loved it so much that every so often, I say "Good night, sweetie (or sweet nerdy)!" to myself (A note on the word "nerdy": I love to be called a nerd, although I would never admit it in person, Ha!)

I don't think I've ever shared my "good night" ritual with anyone before, and I'm glad I did it here.

So here's my pre-quest (or a side-quest, as game designers call additional quests that don't lead you directly or immediately to the win-state of your game) for you before you create your gift to another person, whatever it might become.

Go and take out your favorite cup and make yourself your favorite drink. Then take your favorite treat (or not, if your coffee or tea is already the best treat you can think of), put a flower on a tray with your drink if you have flowers handy in the house, go to the best spot in your home, sit down, or maybe switch on your favorite movie or music first, take your beautiful cup, say to yourself "Mm, this smells great! Thank you for the coffee!" and enjoy your drink.

Then go and diligently wash your cup (or put it in the dishwasher), take all the materials you need to create your gift for a loved one, and play.

***

Torben finished reading the blog post and reread it. The blogger was right. It was time to play. It was time for him to pack all this stuff and move back to Odense. Maybe without letting Karina know. But he would call just in case to make sure she still wanted him to come back.

But first, the pre-quest. Torben felt strange, he realized. He still wasn't sure about the writing thing. He could find other ways to spend his time. For example, the pre-quest, or the side-quest, as the blogger called it. Never really a gamer himself, Torben was still wondering, how just one article, or five if he was honest, had moved him to speak in terms of a game player. In Lily's slang, as he realized, and as it seemed this blogger's too.

OK, let's get my favorite cup. Torben went back to the kitchen and took out the cup he wrapped in paper towel before reading the last Gameful Writing blog post.

He put it on the counter, suddenly startled by a thought, and said aloud to himself, "I know what's missing."

He grabbed his keys and wallet, hurried out of the apartment, locked the door, and went into the twenty-four-hour store across the street. He bought four bars of chocolate. Two were Karina's favorite, milk with white cream and almond crumbs inside, and two of his, dark with puffed rice. Lily claimed that they tasted best together. She used to break a square of each, put them together in her mouth, and chew delightedly.

Torben returned to the apartment. He spread the chocolate bars on the counter into a row like cards and went to brew the coffee for himself.

He brewed the coffee, a bit stronger than usual, the way he liked it most, but rarely permitted himself. Then he took his coffee and one of the chocolate-rice bars and went to the living room. He broke off a square of his bar and put it into his mouth. He started to chew on it, but then he stopped. He let the chocolate melt as he liked doing as a child. When the chocolate melted, he chewed on the remaining and now soft puffed rice, swallowing the sweet mass at the end. Then he sipped his coffee.

Oh, he thought, I forgot to say thank you for the coffee, and chuckled. Then he recalled how Lily made him and Karina laugh even when she wasn't feeling well. Now he realized that even when his daughter was in pain, she wasn't suffering. Whereas he did suffer or thought he did.

There's no need for suffering, but there's a need for love.

Torben wasn't sure what song that was or who sang it. And it didn't really matter. Something else did.

He took his phone and tapped a name on his contact list.

"Karina Larsen speaking."

"Karina, it's Torben."

"Hi Torben, how have you been?"

Torben felt his eyes burning, and he almost recited the usual "I feel miserable" verse. But then he smelled the coffee and tasted chocolate on his tongue and said, "I don't quite understand how it happened, but I am doing better. Much better." He paused. "And I want to come back home. Would this Saturday be all right with you?"

There was a muffled noise on the other end. "This Saturday?" A deep breath. "Yes, yes, sure, it would be all right." Then the muffled noise again.

Torben knew what that noise was. It was the quiet sound of Karina wiping her tears away and sniffing. He hoped these were joyful tears this time. As if reading his thoughts, Karina said, "I'm happy you are coming back so soon."

"I am happy too." And this time, Torben realized that it was easy to allow himself to feel happy that he still had Karina in his life. She was the same person he went with and brought back the most beautiful little girl from faraway China, who was to become the sweetest and the most fantastic daughter in the world, their Lily. He became aware of, or maybe just recalled, that without Karina, he would never have had the treasure of Lily as his daughter in his life. "You know what?" he said, chewing on the next square of his chocolate.

"What?"

"I still have a lot of packing to do, and since there are only two days until Saturday, I gotta go."

Now the muffled noise mixed with laughter. "I love you!"

"I love you too." Torben listened to his wife's quiet laughter and smiled. He put another chocolate square into his mouth.

"What's that noise?" Karina asked. "Are you eating something?"

"Yes," Torben chewed some more before answering. "I'm eating dark chocolate with puffed rice. And drinking coffee."

"Where did you get it?"

"I just bought it."

"You bought yourself your favorite chocolate?"

Torben grinned, "I know, I can't believe it myself."

Then, one of his two favorite sounds of laughter again. "Did you have the decency to buy some for me?"

Torben laughed. It felt so good to be joking with each other again. "I did. But not some of mine. I bought you your favorite."

"Well, then, I think I will take two days off and come to Aalborg tomorrow to help you pack. What do you think?"

"For that, you will get a really special treat. My famous hair-cringing coffee together with a sandwich from squares of our chocolates." He heard a little gasp, smiled, feeling the most special twinge in his heart, and continued. "And each of us will get the treat only after packing a box. I bet I'll end up eating more chocolate than you."

More muffled laugh. "You wish."

After wishing Karina "good night" and a safe drive the next day, Torben opened the blog post on his mobile and scrolled down to the comment area. He wrote his first ever comment:

I am not sure I have earned the writing badge today because I "executed" my gift in the form of chocolate and a telephone call. But you said any form and any material. So I claim it, as well as claiming a badge for the pre-quest. You forgot to announce that one. :) Thank you for what you do! And bless you.

Chapter 6: Lily

*

A door opened, and the head of a nurse appeared, "Lily Larsen?"

Lily started to raise.

Her father stood as well. "Lily, let me at least talk to the doctor and make sure that they don't make any mistakes."

No, her father wasn't going to give in so easily. "Dad!" She almost jumped back into their unfinished discussion that she was old enough to talk to the doctors herself and make sure that they considered her needs and that they'd already met with the doctors. This appointment was not going to provide any additional information. It was about her treatment. There probably wouldn't be a doctor present. And she could go through the procedure herself. And besides, how could her Dad ensure the medical personnel made no mistakes when his knowledge of medicine was as remote as the moon from the earth.

The three other people accompanying her today looked like they were ready to stand and go with her as well. Seriously?

Lily reminded herself that she needed to stay calm. So she took a deep breath and turned to her father, trying to hide the desperation from her voice, "Let's discuss it after, OK? I have to go in there, Dad." She then turned to her mother, Will, and Miriam and said, "Please, stay here or go to the cafeteria together or something. I want to go in there alone."

Lily was sorry that the words didn't sound anything like asking for a favor but more like a hissed order to go to hell, but she needed a break now, and she needed some space for thoughts before starting something that most people hoped they'd never have to do in their lifetimes. "Please!" she repeated emphatically.

She turned away from them and hurried to enter the little room, the door of which the nurse was holding open.

The nurse shook Lily's hand and introduced herself as Clara. Lily didn't catch her surname. The nurse invited Lily to take a chair opposite and then sat down. She took Lily's paperwork and asked her for her date of birth and medical insurance number.

"Did the doctor explain the procedure to you?"

Lilly nodded and started pulling her right sleeve up.

The nurse nodded as well and went on to prepare the injection. "You've got quite a delegation there with you."

"What?" Lily raised her head to look at the nurse, who moved her head toward the door.

Lily frowned. The last thing she needed was small talk with the nurse. "They are not a delegation. They're … my parents, and Will, my boyfriend, and Miriam, my best friend. Miriam is almost like a sister to me." Why was she saying all that to a stranger?

"Like I said, quite a delegation." The nurse with short hair dyed an unnaturally fiery red with several streaks of magenta smiled as she disinfected the spot on Lily's arm where she was about to inject the medicine. "I had quite a delegation myself for my first chemo treatment."

"You had cancer?" Lily glanced at the nurse's name tag to recall her name. Oh, yes, it was Clara.

Clara nodded. "Twice."

Lily opened her eyes wide. "You had cancer twice?" She noticed that the needle was in her skin already. "How? … Are you OK now?"

"Yes, thank you. I'm great now." Clara smiled and pointed at her colorful hair. "I celebrate that with this." She pulled the needle out, put it and the ampule away, and fixed some cotton with a plaster on Lily's arm. "Do you mind if I tell you what helped me?"

Lily shook her head. She wanted to hear everything.

"Trust helped me."

"Trust?"

"Yes, in those who wanted to help me. Trust in myself that I was capable of helping my family and friends to help me."

"I never saw it that way," Lily said. "That they," she nodded as Clara had done toward the people waiting for her outside, "might need my help."

"Oh, they do, more than you think. I was blessed to be inspired by life itself. I got my first cancer diagnosis when I was pregnant with my first child."

Lily gasped as Clara continued, "And I became pregnant naturally after my husband and I had tried all we could to have children, traditional and alternative treatments, in-vitro, too. You name it. When I got a cancer diagnosis during pregnancy, it was like life itself was plotting against me."

Lily pulled her sleeve down and continued to listen.

"But it wasn't. My child was not affected by the chemo, and I went into remission sometime later. Then after the birth of my third child, I got cancer for the second time. For whatever reason, I survived that too."

Clara put her hand on Lily's hand, looked intently into Lily's eyes, and continued. "When you sit there, sick with side effects, life might seem unfair. But what I understood in those moments was that I couldn't explain the so-called bad things that were happening to me, but I couldn't explain those good ones either. Why did I fall pregnant naturally after six years of trying everything we could, and so many failed attempts? How did I get pregnant another two times, when doctors assumed I couldn't, following a difficult first pregnancy and birth? Why did I meet and marry my Australian husband, who came from the other side of the world and was backpacking through Scandinavia when I met him?"

Lily felt the hair on her arms and neck standing up. "I now realize how many lucky and unusual things happened in my life. Starting with my parents coming to China and adopting me."

Clara nodded, gave Lily's hand a gentle squeeze, and withdrew her hand to clean up the table after the treatment. She paused in what she was doing and looked at Lily, her expression thoughtful. "Whenever something challenging happens, try to see what sense or what opportunity it gives you? Getting cancer forced me to do what I really wanted and valued. I finally understood why I became a nurse. So I re-trained as an oncology nurse, to help others in the same situation."

Lily felt herself smiling and giggled, surprising herself. "How many times a day do you share your story?"

Clara laughed, "Fortunately, not every day, but almost every, and not only to cancer patients. I love telling it, as you can see. Thanks for not minding it."

Lily shook her head again. "Thank you. I feel strangely at peace now and can't wait to get out there and come up with ideas for the next days and weeks. It's scary but also feels exciting. Like in a game. I'm a gamer." She smiled apologetically.

"I am too!" Clara grinned.

"Video games? Which ones?"

"No, mostly board games, dice, and cards. I'm one of those old-fashioned types who plays solitaire with a real deck of cards." Clara laughed, then added. "It won't be easy, but easy is boring, as you surely know as a gamer."

Lily smiled and nodded.

Clara put her hand on Lily's again. "You'll do brilliantly, whatever comes your way. Don't you worry! And I have a feeling that you'll come up with something fantastic that will help many people in your life to change their lives from depressing to exciting and inspiring."

Chapter 7: Meetup

* Miriam *

Miriam was one of the first to arrive. The hall at the auditorium was spacious enough to fill a couple of hundred people. She'd never been here before, but she'd been in similar ones at the university.

She was nervous. Following a blog post by an anonymous person and even sharing it was one thing, but coming to a meeting arranged by the person in a separate e-mail newsletter was another.

OK, she told herself. How did the blogger once express it? *"Flip that coin and realize that the nervousness might be excitement."* OK, I'm excited then.

And she had every reason to be excited. In the last six months, since she got the notification of the first blog post and started outlining her book featuring Lily's and her friendship, she had finished writing the book. She'd had it professionally edited too. She had also befriended a graphic designer, who created a brilliant book cover. And finally, Miriam self-published the book after learning how to format the interior of the book all by herself.

Her book wasn't a bestseller, but those who read it loved it. Many of those who read and reviewed the book were strangers to Miriam, but all of her readers wanted more. The relationships she built with some of the book readers through e-mails was nothing short of a miracle and beyond compare with the somewhat cautious chats she used to have in her blog comments, before her writing game adventure began.

Her blogging changed throughout this Gameful Writing adventure too. She enjoyed writing her blog even more than before, and she started sharing her book writing process and her followers tripled.

But something started to bother her now, as the room began filling up. She had seen most of these people before, five years ago, at another gathering. Lily's funeral.

Miriam frowned. Was this some kind of joke? If so, it was a very sick one. She studied the crowd. She would tell the person her opinion as soon as she found him or her.

There was a commotion behind her, and a loud voice asked, "Is this the Gameful Writing meetup?" Several soft answers of "yes" followed.

Miriam turned to find a compactly built young man with short black curly hair. She recognized him as one of Lily's fellow students. What was his name, Tommy, Tony? No, Toni, with an "i." Short for Antonio.

The man stood wide in the entrance blocking the way to others. Miriam noticed Lily's parents and a man in a wheelchair behind them. Was that Will?

As if in answer, the man turned and let people behind him enter. Yes, it was Will! And Lily's supervisor was there too, with what looked like her family.

And Will wasn't alone. He was with someone. Was it his mother?

Was Will behind all this?

Miriam recalled how Will had asked her about featuring the Gameful Writing blog back in February, when she'd picked him up from the airport. Could Will have started the blog and then acted like he didn't know about it? If not, since he was here today, he must have signed up for notifications from the Gameful Writing blogger too. The information on the meetup was only in an email newsletter and not in a blog post. Will didn't even have the decency to let Miriam know that he would be flying to Aalborg to be at this meetup. And Will didn't ask for help this time, did he? Well, he had his mother with him. Of course, Miri thought with disdain. It is evident why he didn't need her help anymore. And he brought not only his mother with him but a whole delegation. It looked like his father was also here. And a younger man who looked like Will and talking to him right now. Probably one of his brothers. Will's whole family had come from England for Lily's funeral, but Miriam couldn't recall now what his brothers had looked like.

Miriam brought her thoughts back to the question that bothered her. Had Will permitted himself to make a joke of something that wasn't a laughing matter? Miriam narrowed her eyes and studied his face. No, he looked as worried and confused as she was.

Miriam looked away from Will and started scanning the gathering crowd from one person to another, trying to understand what was happening here. Just then, Toni smacked an open palm to his forehead and exclaimed, "I can't believe she did this to us, from the afterlife!" He grinned.

First, everyone froze, and then urgent whispers brought one name in waves, "Lily! The e-mails were from Lily! Lily is the Gameful Writing blogger!"

Miriam held her breath. Was it Lily who set this up and planned for all of them to get e-mails five years after her death? Oh, my God!

Now Lily's secretive nature began to make sense. Before her diagnosis, Lily rarely hid her laptop screen from Miriam when she entered the room, but shortly after her first chemo treatment, she began closing her laptop or certain windows more often than not. Lily started keeping secrets. When Miriam once asked what she was doing, Lily answered, "You know how I love games. I started developing my own game, but I'm not ready to show it to anyone yet."

Then Miriam had a flashback of some of the books Lily had on her nightstand. At least some of them were quoted on the Gameful Writing resources page.

The puzzle, as the blogger, Lily, once described her blog, was solved.

** *Will* **

As the still-shocked crowd was spreading through the hall and taking their seats, Will rolled over to one of the windows in the large auditorium. He had to process this new information. Lily had done it all so many years ago and somehow managed to gather them all here today.

Did anyone know? He looked around the room and saw Miriam. Their eyes met, and she nodded. But she had the same expression on her face as him—one of utter surprise.

As if reading his mind, someone asked, "Did anyone know about this project of hers?" Will turned and saw that Lily's supervisor had asked the question.

"I knew, but only a little," Karina, Lily's mother, said from among the cluster of people yet to find a seat. As if on command, those around her, including her husband, moved to give her some space. He hadn't known.

"I'm sorry I didn't tell you," Karina said to Torben, "but I promised Lily I wouldn't. She gave me the id and the codes to make sure that the payments for the domain name, hosting, and the e-mail service continued. During one of her hospital stays, Lily called the dean to ask permission for today's meeting. I only had to call to double-check the room booking was still valid, for the date she had agreed on with the dean and his secretary had recorded."

"Were you on the mailing list?" Will heard himself asking.

All heads turned to look at him. He felt heat rising to his cheeks. He felt a little jealous that Lily hadn't asked him to organize this, but then remembered the state he was in at the time.

Karina nodded, "Yes, I was. But Lily asked me not to let anyone know about her plans before today. She didn't tell me much then about the content of the blog and what the meeting today would be about. So I needed to figure it out — "

Suddenly many phones started bleeping.

*** *Toni* ***

Toni activated his mobile and saw a new mail. A notification for the sixth post of the Gameful Writing blog. He looked around, some had their computers on and were clicking on the link and everyone else was staring at their mobiles.

Hi, and welcome back to the Gameful Writing blog. I'm a bit nervous. No, wait. I am excited. And a little sad, because this is the last blog post. At least for now. Maybe some of you will continue it, if I'm not able to.

Many of you will have figured out who I am by now, especially those who received an e-mail about the first blog post, and if you attended the first Gameful Writing meetup in Aalborg today.

My name is Lily Larsen, and I am an avid gamer, reader, and apparently, also writer, writing all this at the end of 2014. If you are reading this now, then it will be June 2020, and most probably, I am not among you.

That reminds me. Toni, I bet you were the first to figure out who I was.

Toni chewed on his lip and mumbled. "This is scary." But then he grinned, looked at the eyes looking at him, and punched the air. "Yes, I was!"

People smiled, and soft laughter surrounded him.

**** *Sofie* ****

Sofie looked at her husband and daughters sitting next to her. She was so glad she had brought them with her. Her girls of seven and ten looked with big eyes at their father, who was explaining the situation to them in whispers.

"Can someone read the rest of the post out loud?" Someone asked, and Sofie saw that it was one of her students, who, along with Toni and some others, was looking at her.

She smiled, the task of a teacher. "Sure, I'll do it." Sofie got to her feet and read.

I apologize if what I did caused any discomfort. But it was both a selfish wish to be with you after my death and wanting to share with you what I discovered through the experience of living my life, however short it might be in the end.

I had the good fortune to get my first chemo treatment by an amazing nurse with freakishly red hair, who had cancer not once but twice, and gave birth to her first child during her first illness.

There were whispers and gasps around the room. Sofie drew a deep breath herself, waited for the murmur to die down, and then continued to read.

She made me aware that many fantastic people in my life, who would do anything in the world to see me well again, needed support too. They needed support from me. I needed to help them to help me. And I needed to do that in my own way, one I would enjoy. Because we can only bring joy with what we love and enjoy doing. Written words and games are my passion, as some of you know. So Gameful Writing turned out to be my way.

The next few words are for the four people who have accompanied me through the whole journey, including that very first chemo treatment.

Sofie saw the next line in the post and turned to Lily's parents. "Would you like me to continue, or would you prefer to read it for yourselves?"

***** *Torben* *****

Torben noticed the names, Will and Miriam, besides the mention of him and his wife in the remaining text of Lily's last blog post and knew immediately what he had to do.

"I'd like to read the rest out loud." He saw Karina's surprised gaze. He squeezed her hand and pulled her up. "Let's go up front, shall we?" He turned and added, "Will, Miriam, can you please join us?"

Torben caught a glimpse of emotion on Will's face before he looked down and rolled slowly toward the front of the auditorium, after nodding at his mother's encouraging pat on his shoulder. Miriam followed after him.

"Before I continue to read, I would like to apologize to you, Will and Miriam, and to you, darling," he embraced Karina around her shoulders, "for giving you such a hard time five years ago. We all wanted to help Lily, but I know I didn't listen." Torben saw eyes of those present welling up with tears. "But I'm glad we had such great help from Lily. If she's anywhere watching, I know she's laughing happily now." Smiles, tears, and nods followed.

Torben wiped away a stubborn tear and said. "OK, here goes."

After a deep cleansing breath, Torben read.

Mum, Dad, Miriam, and Will! I hope you don't mind if I thank you all together. Even if you might not think so, you still stood together to help me. Even if you told me you failed to understand life and its cruelty to me, I always felt that you shared the beautiful moments with which I was blessed. You laughed at my jokes while holding back tears; you took shifts to be at my side and when accompanying me to chemo. I did notice you arguing, and that you suffered. But you also did everything you could to enrich the moments or to make sure I knew you cared. In your own way, sometimes, sadly, a self-destructive one. But you cared.

Torben noticed how Will's shoulders hung. He withdrew his hand from around Karina and reached out to clap Will on the shoulder. "You cared, Will! And you loved her as nobody else did. Don't be sorry about that." Will hunched further forward, and his shoulders shook softly.

Torben felt Karina gently squeezing his upper arm. He looked at her and nodded. He needed to wait.

Miriam crouched next to Will and rubbed his arm. "Will, are you all right?"

Will straightened, breathing deeply and wiping his eyes. "Yes, yes, thank you!" Then he turned to Torben. "Thank you for what you said. It means a lot to me. And I am also sorry for what happened and how I behaved. You had, no, you *have* an amazing daughter. You will always have her. " He nodded to Torben to continue.

Torben needed a deep breath himself, as did many in the room.

But let's not talk about hard stuff anymore. We bump heads and die in games too. But we don't stay angry or sad there for long. If a game fails to make us happy, we choose another. So let's pick something that uplifts us. If Gameful Writing uplifted you in any way, then I invite you to play and share.

Torben felt someone pulling at his sleeve. It was Karina nodding at Will. Will held a timer out to him. It was set for five minutes. Torben laughed, feeling his face relaxing. He took the timer and nodded for Miriam and Will to take a place at a table in the auditorium. Will placed his wheelchair alongside the first row. Karina walked by him and joined Miriam and him in the first row. Torben followed and looked around the room. Everyone was preparing a notebook, a pen or pencil, a computer, or a mobile to write with. "Everyone ready?" Nods.

Then he turned to Miriam. "Miriam, would you read the countdown, please, and I will start the timer."

Miriam smiled holding her phone, half turned to the rest of the people in the room and said without looking at the blog post on her mobile:

Ready, set, go!

****** *Karina* ******

The timer started bleeping. Karina looked at her husband to her right.

Torben pressed the stop button on the timer and called out, "Stop writing!" Then he added, "Check how many words you've written."

That caused some commotion, along with a few moans. "I have written longhand," a young woman sitting in the middle of the room said. "I definitely have less than those who typed."

Toni stood up. "My name's Toni." He looked at the woman. "You could," he paused visibly trying to pace himself, "just say how many words, approximately," he made two wave-like signs with his right index finger to mimic the approximately equal sign, "you have written, and if you wrote longhand or typed." He sat down again, mumbling something to himself.

Lily's supervisor Sofie stood up next and turned to Toni. "Toni, it's a good idea to introduce ourselves, as some of us won't have met before. My name is Sofie. I used to teach the history of graphic design to Lily, Toni, and some others of you here who studied with Lily. I have the following to say. Let's remember that it's a game we are playing here, and it is about having fun. It's not about the number of words. It's about the gift of Gameful Writing Lily gave to all of us." She looked at Torben and Karina, "I suggest we add up all the words, regardless of how written, and see how many we have managed altogether."

Karina felt excitement and pride stream through her. She stood up and said, "Lily would have loved that." She noticed Torben nodding and smiling. He was already opening the calculator app on his phone.

Karina went to the whiteboard, took the marker, and turned to the room full of people. "Shall we start at the front of the left side, for me, your right side, go back, and then from the back row on the right, sorry, your left side, this one," she gestured, "and to the front. Would that be OK?" Nods were the answer. She almost asked for the word count when she thought of something. Lily would have asked them if they needed time to count the words. Nodding to this thought, Karina asked, "Do you need time to count your words?"

"Two minutes," the same young woman called brightly from her seat with a smile.

Torben set the timer to two minutes and called out, "Two minutes start now."

Karina saw how Torben pressed the start button and took her notes. He looked wordlessly at her with a question in his eyes. Ah, she forgot to count the words she had written. Karina smiled and nodded at him.

As about a third of the heads hung lower over their notes to count the words, and the others looked at their typed text or talked to their neighbors in whispers with soft expressions on their faces, Karina had to smile. "You did something great here, sweetheart," she addressed her daughter in her thoughts. "Thank you for confiding in me and allowing me to witness this."

Karina realized how much she enjoyed standing in front of the audience and being active in all this.

The timer went off. Karina nodded to Torben as he switched the timer off and addressed the room. "I'm ready if you are." Smiles and chuckles were the answer.

Torben signaled that he would start. "Darling, you wrote 129 words. Not bad for longhand, I would say. I wrote only 132, but I typed on my phone, please observe." Laughter followed.

Karina wrote 129 on the board and then 261, adding both numbers Torben named. For the following half an hour, Karina listened, repeated the numbers, calculated, wrote down the intermediate results, wiped and corrected the mistakes, laughing along with those who helped her to add up. Two children present in the room excitedly reported that they wrote twenty-three and forty-one words, respectively. Miriam and Will were the last to share their results.

The result was 38,383. Karina gazed at the number and read it into the stunned silence around her. "Thirty-eight thousand, three hundred, and eighty-three. Wow, what a number!" Karina turned to face everyone in the room. "Lily would have been over the moon, seeing that number."

"She'd probably start theories on how five, her favorite number played into it," Will said, smiling.

Miriam nodded, chuckling and half turned in her chair to face the others. "Yes, she would. Lily would have probably pointed out that this is a five-digit number and that the difference between the neighboring digits in each pair is five. She saw the number five everywhere. And she would've performed a little dance after noticing the symmetry in this number." Everyone laughed.

As the laughter died, Karina noticed the melancholy on everybody's face. Was this the end of Gameful Writing? She had an idea, but there was something she needed to know first. Lily would have wanted to know it too. "I have a question for all of you. What did Gameful Writing mean to you? Did it change anything? Did it maybe change something in you?"

There were nods, and Karina thought someone raised a hand when Torben asked loudly, for everyone to hear, "What did it mean for you, Karina?" He looked directly at her. Was he angry that she hadn't confided in him that she knew more than anyone else in the room, even if only a little, of what Lily was up to?

She hesitated but saw that everyone awaited her answer. She owed it to all of them. She looked around the room and then at Torben. "I've learned so much during this half a year. Even more than in the past five. I asked Lily why she chose this year for the blog to go live and for this meeting to occur, and she said, '2020 is a fun number.' Yes, having fun even in the most difficult situations, even when I felt utterly sad, was what Lily taught me. Fun is happening in the experience of now, in all senses. So I experienced waiting, learning, fearing, losing, gaining, forgiving myself, Torben, and others, and so much more during these years."

Karina turned to Miriam and Will and then looked at where Will's family sat and smiled. Will's mother smiled back. Karina felt her eyes welling up and took a deep breath to be able to continue. "I also discovered so much during the past half-year since Gameful Writing went live. I re-discovered my dream to be there for Torben, even if we weren't always together during the past five years, and to go for this dream even if it meant giving

Torben time and space to feel and experience his grief. I also learned that there were things I needed to say to him, and I did. Then there were things I thought I didn't want or need to do, sometimes at work, only finding out that I both needed and wanted them. My work again became so rewarding and crisp, maybe even more so than when I first got the position a couple of years ago. I also learned why I do what I do, both in my personal and work life. And I learned to treat myself and those I care about with kindness."

Karina looked at Torben and noticed that the hard expression he'd had when he challenged her to talk had disappeared. Warmth glittered along with tears in his eyes, and he smiled. "But most of all, I learned to see things in a new light. First of all, of course, writing. I never thought of classifying writing into types, as Lily did in her first post. Did you?" she asked and looked around the room.

Everyone shook their heads.

"But these types make so much sense, don't they?"

Nods and several calls of "yes" came in answer.

"I discovered these types apply not only to writing but to anything we are up to. But of course, I learned that I could and sometimes even enjoy writing. I've never told anyone before, but I started writing a diary." She looked at Torben, and he looked back, surprised but also delighted.

"Yes, to see and approach things gamefully, and take ownership of that like game designers do when they adjust their game designs so that the players of their games, who include themselves, have the most fun possible, is the biggest discovery of all. That it is possible, even in the hardest of situations." Karina turned to Torben, "And I realized all of that just now while speaking. Thank you for challenging me. I wouldn't have otherwise." She watched Torben shifting uncomfortably in his chair and smiled at him then turned to the audience. "Do you remember how Lily challenged us to write under a table or in a kitchen sink?"

"I do," Toni called out, and everyone laughed. He stood up, "No, seriously, I will never forget that. I thought it was utterly stupid, but I still did it, because, despite all its ridiculousness or maybe because of it, the challenge made me curious about what writing could offer. I thought I hated it before. Now," he looked up and then around, "and I hate to admit that Lily also won this round of our constant rivalry, I love writing. It's a big part of my job now. I write articles for a magazine, for heaven's sake!" They all laughed, and Karina noticed how Lily's and Toni's supervisor Sofie clasped her mouth and tried to suppress her giggles. Then she wiped her tears, only giving way to more laughs. Toni pointed at her and grinned. "Could you ever believe this would happen?"

"No," Sofie replied through more laughter. The two girls sitting between her and a man who grinned at Toni watched this exchange with curiosity and amusement. "Would you re-write your master's thesis now?" Sofie asked and laughed again.

"I wouldn't go that far," Toni said, grimaced and laughed in the next moment too, sat down, and called out to Karina, "Sorry, I interrupted you."

Karina felt the ease that was spreading through the room and said, "You didn't. You just answered my question." She paused. Then she had an idea. "So, did I complete my challenge?" She turned to Torben.

He grinned. "You did. You reached Level Six of your writing or self-discovery game."

Karina grinned back. "Yes!" She pumped a fist in the air through the waves of laughter and cheers. Then she felt mischievousness rising in her. "But you, people, didn't. So stand up and say what Gameful Writing did for you." She went back to her seat and watched how people one by one stood and told their stories.

Toni had become the "ranting editor," as he called himself, at Choose The News as well as the head of the Italian branch of this young and fast-growing company. He was dividing his time between Aalborg and Rimini, where he came from. "This summer seems to be turning out pretty well in Aalborg, so I plan to stay here, and when the darkness comes back, I will flee to Rimini more often," he announced with a grin on his face.

Sofie had finished writing and submitted her Ph.D. thesis, and the initial feedback was fantastic and very encouraging. She was busy with more research on the topic of hope and how it was represented in graphic design throughout history. Her colleagues at the University and internationally supported and encouraged her research.

Miriam told them about the book she wrote and devoted to Lily. She also shared that she was writing a sequel. She shyly but proudly showed her first book to the audience. And blushed, when Karina took a copy out of her purse and said, "Would you please sign this copy for Torben and me?" Karina saw the delight in Miriam's eyes and added, "If you need anything for your research for the sequel about Lily, just let us know." Miriam forced out, "Thank you!" through the tears.

Will raised his hand and told everyone how the second blog post had affected him, and how he revealed the reason behind his wheelchair to his employees and the world. Everyone held their breath as he recounted his attempted suicide, consequent recovery, and creation of the company. Smiles and tears returned when he told how they got more brilliant employees in their company after his confession. These new colleagues had themselves attempted suicide at least once in their lives, but were now keen to help others to go through tough times without endangering themselves. He said that the company name, Inclusivity Testing Repair & Upgrade, had taken on an entirely new meaning, and, in addition to what they did before, they now facilitated meetings to help those who were unable to see the light at the end of the tunnel. "A gameful attitude is such light," he said, "and I should have known that Lily was behind all that. She was and is such a light." He looked at Karina and smiled.

She smiled back and was interrupted from her warm reverie by Torben, who stood up beside her and spoke.

"I must admit that Gameful Writing didn't change my writing habits." He chuckled along with people around him, then he turned and took Karina's hands in his. She felt goosebumps on her arms. "And it hasn't changed me as a person. I am the same grumpy, competitive, procrastinating man I've always been. Yes, consider it a repetition of the warning I made so many years ago when we married." Karina couldn't stop gazing into his eyes. "But it still changed my life. Mostly because I didn't have to change. Gameful Writing and each of the posts, but especially the fifth one about writing or expressing as a gift, brought me back to the present moment and an awareness of what I treasure most. And whom I treasure most." Karina felt how Torben squeezed her hands, and she let her tears spill onto her cheeks.

Torben bowed forward and said quietly to her, "Sorry, darling, I had to say it, after I challenged you so rudely before. I'm sorry."

Karina laughed through her tears and kissed Torben's cheek. "No need to say sorry." Then she gently pulled Torben to sit, wiped her tears away, and watched a man in the back row standing up to report about his experiences of the writing game.

The door opened, and a woman entered before the man could say anything. "I'm sorry to interrupt." She seemed to search the room, so Karina stood up and waved to her. The man in the back row sat down. As soon as the woman, who stood in the opened door, saw Karina, she said, "I need to leave in half an hour, or an hour at most, lock up and set the alarm for the building. Do you need much longer?"

Karina reached into her pocket for her mobile and checked the time. Had it only been a couple of hours since they entered this room? It felt like a lifetime ago. Karina looked back at the woman. "May we have half an hour to wrap up?"

The woman nodded and disappeared.

Karina felt the urgency of the idea that occurred to her before. "Before we go, let's agree on how to go on from here. I don't want Gameful Writing to end."

The room filled with increasing noise. "Me neither." "I want it to continue, but how?" "Lily is not here." "She'd know." "But she's not here."

Karina raised her right hand and waited until everyone went quiet again and turned to her.

"May I say something?" Will interrupted.

Karina nodded.

"I just heard some people wondering how to go on from here, but Lily said it clearly in her last post today." Will backed his wheelchair away from the front row he was sitting at and turned to face everyone. "Just recall, she wrote… Just a second." He paused to take his mobile out and open the window containing Lily's last blog post. "Here it is. '*If Gameful Writing uplifted you in any way, then I invite you to play and share.*'"

"Yeah, but how?" Someone called from the back.

"Let's create a group of those who would be interested in maintaining the Gameful Writing page and blog," Torben stood up. "We as parents," he put his arm around Karina, "will form part of it."

Karina nodded when she saw Torben turning to her for approval. "Yes, we'll do anything to help. If someone could take on updating the design, the content of the resources and writing and posting for the blog, that would be wonderful."

"I'll take the design," Toni called out. "And an occasional ranting post." He grinned.

"I'll work on the resources and books, especially those on anthropology and kaizen." Sofie stood up and said, "But I will need help with the books and resources on the writing craft, as well as everything about games."

"I can do that," Miriam called out. "Especially the writing part."

"I'll take the games and gamification part," Will said.

"I have an idea for the blog." The young woman who previously sat in the middle of the room and complained about writing longhand, now stood beaming. "I'm following a writing blog where writers share the weekdays and post something every week. There are so many of us here, if each volunteer wrote something once a month, we would have daily posts. I'd gladly coordinate." She turned to Karina. "What if everyone here who'd like to write something for the blog emails blogger@gamefulwriting.com, and you pass on their names and addresses to me, then I will have a go at scheduling the posts? Oh, I forgot to say." The woman giggled. "My name is Tanya."

Karina was overwhelmed by all the inspiration and warmth that ran through the room, and all she could do was nod.

She could see now that this group, and maybe even a bigger one, would meet again before too long. And that there might even be many small group meetings. She didn't know. She just knew that her daughter had helped many people in this room to find joy and happiness for themselves. She heard herself whispering, "Thank you, Lily!"

Hugs and smiles were exchanged as people said their goodbyes or agreed to go for coffee together somewhere on this Saturday afternoon, and Karina and Torben stood hand in hand, waiting for the room to empty.

Karina heard how many who left turned to look around the room and said or mouthed the same phrase she had whispered to her long gone but ever so present daughter a couple of minutes before, "Thank you, Lily!"

Karina wiped the numbers off the board, but not before Torben had taken a picture of it, then they both walked along some of the rows to check that all was in order and left the room.

Karina discovered a group of people waiting for them. Will, his family, Miriam, Toni, Sofie with her husband and, yes, this must have been her two daughters, and Tanya. Will's mother looked into Karina's eyes and said, smiling brightly, "We thought we could agree on the design for Gameful Writing right away, before you leave for Odense and we take our flight to London tomorrow morning. Would you have time for a coffee and dinner?"

Karina searched Torben's face for his opinion, and seeing his answer clearly, she smiled and said, "We couldn't wish for more."

The End

Gameful Writing - Summary of Writing Types and Lessons Learned

Five Types of Writing

Type 1: The books or stories we want to write, but fear the outcome of.

Type 2: The articles, reports, or other pieces we need to write, but fret over the feedback.

Type 3: The pieces we have committed to writing, but which we neither want nor consider it necessary to write.

Type 4: Writing and researching to explore ourselves, to find our truth in what we do.

Type 5: Writing as a gift, or, in other words, writing to create something for others or our future selves to enjoy.

Victoria Ichizli-Bartels

Lessons Learned

Lesson 1: Start playing. You won't experience the game unless you play it. Whatever the game is, play it, don't think it!

Lesson 2: When you need to say something, tell it like it is. And go to Lesson 1.

Lesson 3: Add ridiculous rules to your challenge. You don't need to take it too seriously, but to find the fun in it right away.

Lesson 4: There is part of you in everything. Let your curiosity (gut) lead you.

Lesson 5: To be kind to others, start by being kind to yourself. If you want to create the best ever gift for someone, make a small gesture, gift, or treat for yourself now.

Lesson 6: Trust yourself, others, and life. You might not know the outcome of what you are doing or going through, but you have full control of this moment because there's always a choice in every moment of our lives. Your compasses in how to treat yourself and others are kindness, honesty, helpfulness, and joy. Remember that not all unexpected things are wrong or necessarily bad. Many of them turn out to meet or even exceed our expectations.

Lesson 7: Be open to seeing anything in a new, gameful light and be willing to have fun. And don't forget the design part, because the design (or analysis, which you could see as the design adjustment) part is a game of its own. You are both the designer (or at least the co-designer) and the player (co-player) of all your real-life games. Here, Gameful Writing and its lessons come full circle. Lily said the following in her first blog post in chapter 1, section **: "*Remember, FUN is your compass. Always have it handy.*"

Why I Wrote This Book

How I started turning writing into a fun game

Today, I gamify my life and help others to turn their lives into fun games. It wasn't planned and happened more or less by itself, but I am utterly grateful it did. Doing so might even be my life's mission.

The very first part of my life that I gamified (i.e., turned into games) — even before I knew that there was a term, "gamification," for bringing game elements and mechanisms into real-life contexts — was writing.

Being an avid reader, at some point I started to wonder if I could write something interesting too. I started diving into books and blogs about the craft of writing, and I found out what many aspiring writers hear when they begin their adventure: that writing is a difficult job. I would certainly agree with that. Undoubtedly, writing a book is not a one-day assignment. It takes weeks, months, or even years.

That is why, at first, I decided to write short pieces and share them on my blog. I wanted to share my writing immediately after creating something. Starting a blog was the solution.

But there was a story inside me that wanted to be told. One that couldn't be told in just a short blog post. It needed an entire book. And being dear to my heart – it was the story of my late father trying to locate the family he lost during World War II – the story kept reminding me that I needed to tell it.

Around this time, I read a German translation of the book *Writing Down the Bones* by Natalie Goldberg and found there the following words:

"Write what disturbs you, what you fear, what you have not been willing to speak about. Be willing to be split open."

So, like many people before me, I realized I wanted to write that book with my whole heart. And like so many others too, I felt I didn't have the time to do it.

What was I to do?

I decided I would start writing it without putting any pressure on myself to finish it. I would just test out how it felt to write and see where it might lead.

I wrote a few chapters, then shared them with a friend and my niece. They loved what they read. But then I stopped writing the story. Reasons for it were plenty, and all the typical culprits. Full-time job, a family with a small child, voluntary work, the story being too sad, and my telling of the story too slow, thinking it wasn't good enough, etc., etc.

Joining a writing course with my dear friend and best-selling author Menna van Praag helped to boost my energy for writing again. Every month for about a year, I sent her three pages of the story and then got her feedback both in written form and on the phone during a one-hour telephone seminar, together with her other students.

Just a few months into the course, and particularly in between the monthly phone calls, my writing energy would ebb again. My fellow students and I complained to Menna that we couldn't find the time to write, so Menna suggested playing a game. She proposed that each of us write for just a few minutes a day for a month, and share our experiences in the Facebook group created by one of the students.

It was a fantastic experience. We cheered each other through the process, and my writing just flew. Sometimes I only wrote for five minutes or less, but still, it was progressing. In the subsequent months, I forgot about the game, but I continued to write and to feel its positive effects. I suspect that I was still turning bits of my writing process into a game without recording the points. After all, I did have a feedback system in the form of word count, and chapters reviewed and edited.

Writing my first book healed many wounds. I found that my father's story was a beautiful one, with some sad moments but also joyful ones, and all of them deep and unique.

It also brought my mother and me closer together. We shared many beautiful moments as I asked her about my father and his story.

Writing and sharing my first book will always remain an unforgettable experience. I tasted the joy and magic of creating, and I witnessed the effect my creation had on others. It ignited something very personal. I saw people smile and heard from my mother how pleasantly surprised our relatives in Moldova were when they found out about my first book. She told me about the hugs they gave her and the memories they shared with her about my father.

Sharing the writing game with others

In 2015, even with two small children, I managed to finish my first book: revising it, having it professionally edited, and then publishing it. Doing all of it in small steps between taking care of my family, maintaining a household, and blogging.

At the end of that year, I published another book. Shortly before that, I joined a writers' club in Aalborg, Denmark, where I live. At that time, I was already working on several writing projects in parallel, continuing the voluntary work in a technical community, moved to a new house with my family, and had started a business. At some point, my fellow writers in the writers' club asked me how I managed to pursue so many projects in parallel, along with taking care of a business and a family with two small children.

As I was contemplating how to summarize and explain how I did it, I recalled the game introduced to me by Menna. So, I suggested that my friends give it a go. I organized a Facebook group called "Procrastination Breakers Club," where we played this game with rounds going for one month.

The rules of the game were straightforward. We had to introduce the project we wanted to take into the game. It didn't have to be writing; it could be learning a language, practicing a musical instrument, planning a big event, such as a wedding, working out, renovating a house, or anything else that we wanted or had to do but didn't think we had time for. Then we had to pursue the project for at least five minutes a day. If we did it, we earned a point. If we didn't, then we lost the point to our procrastinating selves. And if we persevered for less than five minutes, we got half a point with the other half going to the procrastinating part of ourselves.

At the end of the month, we counted up our points, and if it was a writing project, we also counted the words we had written.

That first round of the game I moderated for the Procrastination Breakers' Club was one of the most significant revelations in my life as a writer. In that month, I wrote more than six thousand words, by writing for five minutes a day, sometimes more (but never longer than twenty minutes) and sometimes less. Six thousand! If I continued to write the book at the same pace, I would have a full manuscript within a year. By writing for only five minutes a day!

Many traditionally published authors sign contracts with publishers where they commit to writing one book a year. So, by writing in small chunks every day, I would be able to write a manuscript a year and manage such terms too.

That was one of the most beautiful discoveries for me as a writer.

I didn't proceed with that book further but finished writing and published several other books of various lengths that year and in the years after.

And another marvelous thing happened. During one of the rounds of our game, a writer friend wrote me a personal message on Facebook. She told me that a sentence I often like quoting and which I mentioned at the writers' panel we both attended helped her to break her writer's block. She was late with sending a book manuscript to her publisher, and it seemed unlikely that she would manage to get it done. The sentence she referred to was: "You can't edit an empty page."

[A side-note: I was thrilled to discover sometime later that one of my all-time favorite pearls of wisdom for writers originates from my all-time favorite fiction writer. Here is the original version of this brilliant bit of wisdom: "You can't edit a blank page." — Nora Roberts]

I was delighted when this author friend shared this experience with me, and I invited her to play the game with us. She accepted the invitation.

She commented on the page of our group that the game was helping her, and she expressed her surprise with much color and enthusiasm. Sometime later, she posted a message with multiple exclamation marks announcing that she had finished the manuscript and sent it to her publisher.

This author's name is Sasha Christensen, and she is an award-winning Young Adult fantasy author in Denmark. She allowed me to quote her and even suggested that I put the cover of her book (the one she'd been struggling to finish) on my website. Before sending the picture, she wrote, "This [book] is the one you helped break my block on, btw ;)."

Seeing the effect the game could have, and how much fun could come of it, I decided to dedicate a little book to it, which I named *5 Minute Perseverance Game*. The board game I got from my husband as a gift for Christmas the previous year inspired me to structure this little book as if it were the description for such a game. Writing this little book was a unique and fun experience in itself.

After that, I turned all of my book projects (seventeen to date, including the free e-books on my website and excluding this one) into games, including all aspects, such as revisions before and after the professional edit, publishing, marketing, and many more. Writing this book was no exception, and I don't expect any future books to be either.

Apart from writing, I turn all projects, activities, and aspects of my life into fun games. Ever since discovering the following quote, I understood why and how that was possible.

"What defines a game are the goal, the rules, the feedback system, and voluntary participation. Everything else is an effort to reinforce and enhance these four core components." — Jane McGonigal, *Reality Is Broken*

I am sure you will agree that goals, rules, feedback, and the will to participate (which includes the free choice to leave a game) in a project or activity are inherent to anything we are up to. Along with the gifts of anthropology (awareness and engagement), and kaizen (small steps), this truth about games and projects is part of why I love discovering how I can design and play various project and activity games in my life.

About this book

Gameful Writing is Book 4 in the "Gameful Life" series.

Writing it was unique for me because ever since writing my first book and playing the writing game for the first time, working on my books has been my favorite kind of project game.

I started writing the book on gameful writing even before books one to three in the "Gameful Life" series. Ever since coming up with the idea for the series, I knew I would devote at least one book to approaching writing gamefully.

When I was writing my motivational book for writers, *Cheerleading for Writers*, I recalled a trinket I bought for myself back in 2013 to remind me that I am living my writing dream. It is a chain and a locket in the shape of a little book, with the words "FAIRY TALE" written in capital letters on its cover. I saw this locket in a jewelry shop at Copenhagen international airport, after writing a few pages of my first novel, while waiting for my plane home. As soon as I saw this metal bead shaped like a tiny book, I thought, wow, I am writing a book. I am a writer. I can't believe this. That is a fairy tale!

I wear this chain and the pendant nearly every day.

Here is how I finished the chapter in *Cheerleading for Writers*, where I mentioned the locket:

So I live my fairy tale now.

And when I am self-editing, I am separating ashes from lentils.

I am not at the "And they lived happily ever after" yet because this would mean being at the end of my fairy tale.

Do I want this?

No!

Right now, I will just enjoy every moment, whether it is removing the ashes or dancing at a ball.

After writing and publishing seventeen books, I still sometimes can't believe that I am a writer and an author.

When I am in the process of writing, it does feel like a fairy tale and often like playing my favorite game. I need to put some effort in to level-up, but that effort feels utterly fun and what I want to do in that moment. Nowadays, having tapped into the power of this creative game of self-expression, I often find myself writing (or reading, which fuels my well of creativity) almost any time I have a couple of minutes to myself or am waiting for someone.

Gameful writing was the start of my gameful life, and I will always cherish this experience.

This book initially had a completely different shape than it does today. I have this experience with each of my books. The plotting and planning of the book project might take one form, but when I actually *play* the writing game, the result is always different and always better. Better because it is tangible and real and not like day-dreams about the book, diffuse, unclear, and full of fears about how it would turn out.

I wrote this book in the form of a parable where characters learn something along the way.

I was inspired to write some of my books in the form of a parable when I read modern parables on how to have success in business and life, as well as how to become financially independent.

I had read a couple of parables in the past, *Who Moved My Cheese?* by Spencer Johnson, is one of the most recent, but I had long forgotten about them.

I rediscovered this genre not that long ago. It was after I published the book *Cheerleading for Writers*, which I mentioned and quoted above. Since this book is for writers, I was curious about what the writers who read my book were writing. One of the reviewers was the New York Times bestselling author John David Mann. The *Go-Giver* books, which he co-authored with Bob Burg, sounded very intriguing, and I ended up reading all of them, as well as the other parables he co-wrote with other authors.

I loved the idea of writing a fiction story that featured true feelings and experiences, and that taught life lessons.

Initially, I thought to have one character, who learns from one mentor, but that changed too. I ended up with seven characters, each of them learning something along the way (including the mentor). I ended up classifying writing into different types, but not in terms of different styles or genres. I found myself defining them according to the feelings and thoughts we have and behavior we show toward multiple writing projects and assignments, which we either want or have to do, or both.

Writing, and especially writing on my works-in-progress, including this one here, has a healing and empowering effect on me. It is one of my ultimate boosters for a good mood, well-being in general, the experience of fun, curiosity, passion, and courage. That is why the healing and empowering effect of writing runs like a red thread throughout this book, and the addition of the gameful approach enhances the effect so that it becomes ever so fantastic.

The following scenario loomed in my head while I was working on this book. If any of us was present at a funeral and a child who lost their loved one was completely upset, what would many of us do to help brighten their day at least a little and take the child's mind off their loss? Many of us would suggest playing a game, wouldn't we? Maybe a quiet one, but there would be an idea of one or even more games for the child to choose from and to put their attention on something light and joyful. We can do the same for ourselves in any moment we perceive as challenging. Games and what inspires them are always there for us to tap into.

I hope you enjoyed reading this book as much as I enjoyed writing it. I thoroughly loved playing this writing game. And I hope you enjoy designing and playing your writing and life games too!

Credits

Studying Oneself as an Anthropologist Would Do

Award-winning authors, Ariel and Shya Kane suggest something quite brilliant in their award-winning books, radio show *Being Here,* and live seminars. They invite the readers, listeners, and participants of their workshops to study themselves, those around them, and the circumstances they are in as *anthropologists* would do, non-judgmentally.

This suggestion is utterly simple and at the same time extremely profound.

"Practice your anthropological approach. Pretend you're a scientist observing a culture of one — yourself. The trick is not to judge what you see, but to neutrally observe how you function, including your thought processes. Awareness and kindness are key." — Ariel and Shya Kane, *How to Have A Match Made in Heaven*

This idea inspired me to write the following paragraphs in Lily's first blog post (chapter 1: Miriam, section **):

But let's start with the first level of our writing game: the books or stories we want to write, but are afraid of for some reason. What can help in this situation?

Firstly, becoming aware of your wish. Allowing yourself to have it. How do you do that, you ask?

Do it like an anthropologist would, when studying an interesting culture. You are a fascinating culture of one, exposed to many fascinating collective cultures, absorbing and mixing and sometimes boiling those juices into a very personal cocktail.

The Writing Game Variant with Dice

The variant with the dice in chapter 1: Miriam, section **, was inspired by an interview I did with my dear friend and writer Naz Ahsun for her podcast, "The Inspired Writer Podcast[1]." I had the honor of appearingon the first episode to talk about turning life into fun games. In the second half of the interview (16:10 of 26:22 min), Naz had the idea of rolling dice to figure out how many sentences to write next.

Here is how I used this idea in Lily's first blog post:

---

[1] https://www.youtube.com/watch?v=iz9rfOd0Uis

So, here is the playful variant this time. Take a dice (or more than one, if you want to write for longer), or open a dice app online and roll the dice. You can also decide to ignore one or other of the small numbers and roll again. Or total all the points after rolling three times, or add those on the multiple dice, if you play (yes, this is part of the game too!) with more than one at a time. It is your choice. But when you have rolled the number of times you decided (you could also determine this number with a roll of the dice, just once I would say ;)), then set your timer to this time and play.

Here is another idea: you can choose that the number you roll is how many sentences you must write in this round. Choose whatever feels best (or most fun) for you. The only mistake you can make is not giving it a try. I am super glad that I did.

The Spotlight

The figurative "spotlight" in Lily's third blog post (chapter 3: Toni, section **) was inspired by a story told by Ariel and Shya Kane in their acclaimed book *Practical Enlightenment*.

Here is the extract from Lily's third blog post:

What I see now but didn't see when my family, friends, and I found out that I had cancer, is that we all competed to show how sad and miserable we were about it. Only when I turned the figurative "spotlight" away from myself and from how I thought I felt, and just listened to my loved ones, only then did I see that they were scared of what it would be like to lose me.

And here is Ariel's memorable account of wearing a headlamp, from *Practical Enlightenment*:

"Whatever direction I turned my gaze, the headlamp automatically followed since it was strapped to my head and wherever I turned my attention, the view was illuminated. Then the light accidentally slipped, pivoted down into my eyes and I was blinded. It was a simple matter of readjusting the direction of the beam so I could go about packing my things.

 "… I realized that it is as if we have each been equipped with a personal headlamp that illuminates things. We see whatever we direct our attention to, allowing us to take care of the things and the people in the world around us. However, if our 'light' slips and we focus on ourselves and how we're doing, we become virtually blind and lose our way. *With awareness, it's a simple matter of readjusting the direction of the beam away from our complaints, worries or thinking about ourselves and bringing*

it back to this moment of now and the world around us." —
Ariel and Shya Kane, *Practical Enlightenment*

Golf as an Example of Unnecessary and Voluntary Obstacles in Games

The more I read about games and gamification, the more I encounter golf being used as an example of how rules contribute to the engagement and fun factor of the whole process. I used this example, extending it to other games, in chapter 3: Toni, section **.

Here is the excerpt from Lily's third blog post:

I bet you know more than one person who plays either badminton, hockey, tennis, ping-pong, baseball, cricket, or golf. And yet, in all these games, none of the players who want to win the game would do the straightforward and most logical thing, which is to go and grab that little object they all hunt for or throw around, and put it in the goal net, small hole, or onto the opponent's field. Instead, every one of them willingly and dutifully takes a hockey stick, a bat, a club, or a racket and hits or hunts for that little, tiny object with all their might and skill. They do all that to win that match of their favorite game, regardless of how small or big the prize might be.

And the following quote inspired it:

"As a golfer, you have a clear goal: to get a ball in a series of very small holes, with fewer tries than anyone else. If you weren't playing a game, you'd achieve this goal the most efficient way possible: you'd walk right up to each hole and drop the ball in with your hand. What makes golf a game is that you willingly agree to stand really far away from each hole and swing at the ball with a club. Golf is engaging exactly because you, along with all the other players, have agreed to make the work more challenging than it has any reasonable right to be." — Jane McGonigal, *Reality Is Broken*

The Ridiculous Challenge

Here is my inspiration for the additional "ridiculous" challenge in chapter 3: Toni, section **. That is, the suggestion of writing under a table or in the kitchen sink.

Here are the two suggestions from Lily's third blog post:

So, if you want to win this round of the writing game, then here's the ridiculous rule for you.

Get all the gadgets, take all of them under your desk or table, and write.

…

The only variant I will allow here is if you choose to write in a place that is as or even more ridiculous than sitting under a table. Like sitting in the kitchen sink, for example.

The first, writing under a table, was inspired by a challenge my son got in school, to promote daily reading and make it more fun. This scheme included various ideas for where or how the pupils should read, including under a table, sitting outside, in the dark, under a duvet, and many others.

In 2016, I taught a seminar with the title "Exploring the meaning of Write-What-You-know in Fiction" at a Creative Writers Camp organized by the South Gate School of Creative Writing in Aalborg. At one point in this seminar, I gave all participants a prompt to write freely for five minutes. I joined the challenge. Before the workshop, I searched for fun first sentences online and found a website listing the first lines of one hundred novels. There, one caught my attention immediately. It was "I write this sitting in the kitchen sink" by Dodie

Smith from *I Capture the Castle* (1948). It sounded utterly unusual and fun.

The reaction from the twenty-five participants of the workshop was colorful; many were surprised, amused, some skeptical. But the results were fantastic. We all read our pieces aloud. None of them was lacking. All contained terrific ideas, some reflective and some humorous, but all brilliant. That was an unforgettable experience for me as an instructor, and I often share the story of this free-writing exercise. I'm glad I got to use it here in this book as well.

Agatha Christie and Washing Dishes

Chapter 4: Sofie, section **, Lily's fourth blog post:

You could also go for a walk. Or you could wash the dishes like Agatha Christie was famous for doing, where she claimed to get her best ideas.

I found several accounts of Agatha Christie claiming to get her best ideas while doing the dishes.

The "Quote Investigator" addresses this "rumor" and quotes an answer by Christie to the following question in an interview in "New York Times" in 1966[2]:

Question: "How do you concoct whodunits that have rolled up world sales of 300-million copies?"

Answer: "Walking or just washing up, a tedious process. Years ago I got my plots in the tub, the old-fashioned, rim kind — just sitting there thinking, undisturbed, and lining the rim with apple cores." — Agatha Christie

---

[2] https://quoteinvestigator.com/tag/agatha-christie/

Recommended Reading

The parables that inspired me and ignited a wish to write some in the "Gameful Life" series:

- *The Go-Giver: A Little Story About a Powerful Business Idea*, Bob Burg and John David Mann, 2010

- *The Go-Giver Influencer: A Little Story About a Most Persuasive Idea*, Bob Burg and John David Mann, 2018

- *The Go-Giver Leader: A Little Story About What Matters Most in Business*, Bob Burg and John David Mann, 2016

- *The Latte Factor: Why You Don't Have to Be Rich to Live Rich*, David Bach, and John David Mann, 2019

- *The Recipe: A Story of Loss, Love, and the Ingredients of Greatness*, Charles M. Carroll and John David Mann, 2017

The parables on writing and self-publishing that I have discovered and read so far:

- *A Tale of Two Authors: Your Choices Define Your Future*, Sean M. Platt, 2019

- *The Writer's Block (The Short Story Collection Series)*, Michael Priv, 2017

- *The Short, Spectacular Indie-Publishing Career of Matilda Walter: A Short Story*, Sandra Hutchison, 2014

I read all the fantastic books by Ariel and Shya Kane again and again. They are the kindest and most enlightening awareness boosters I have discovered so far:

- *Being Here: Modern Day Tales of Enlightenment*, Ariel and Shya Kane, 2007

- *Being Here...Too: Short Stories of Modern Day Enlightenment*, Ariel and Shya Kane, 2018

- *How to Create a Magical Relationship: The 3 Simple Ideas that Will Instantaneously Transform Your Love Life*, Ariel and Shya Kane, 2008

- *How to Have A Match Made in Heaven: A Transformational Approach to Dating, Relating, and Marriage*, Ariel and Shya Kane, 2012

- *Practical Enlightenment*, Ariel and Shya Kane, 2015

- *Working on Yourself Doesn't Work: The 3 Simple Ideas That Will Instantaneously Transform Your Life*, Ariel and Shya Kane, 2008

To make progress in small steps and to bypass my fears, I read:

- *One Small Step Can Change Your Life: The Kaizen Way*, Robert Maurer, 2014

- *Mastering Fear: Harnessing Emotion to Achieve Excellence in Work, Health and Relationships*, Robert Maurer, 2016

- *The Spirit of Kaizen: Creating Lasting Excellence One Small Step at a Time*, Robert Maurer, 2012

To learn from others who turn their health (and other big) challenges into games or use game elements (such as count-down) to practice everyday courage, I read:

- *SuperBetter: The Power of Living Gamefully*, Jane McGonigal, 2015

- *The 5 Second Rule: Transform Your Life, Work, and Confidence with Everyday Courage*, Mel Robbins, 2017

The quote at the beginning of this book is from the following brilliant book. The whole book is worth reading:

- *The Mental Game of Writing: How to Overcome Obstacles, Stay Creative and Productive, and Free Your Mind for Success*, James Scott Bell, 2016

More great books on the writer's mindset:

- *The Successful Author Mindset: A Handbook for Surviving the Writer's Journey (Books for Writers 4)*, Joanna Penn, 2016

- *The 10X Author: Level Up or Be Left Behind (Stone Tablet Singles Book 2)*, Sean M. Platt and Johnny Truant, 2019

- *Level Up: Quests to Master Mindset, Overcome Procrastination and Increase Productivity*, Rochelle Melander, 2019

Acknowledgments

First of all, dear reader, thank you very much for purchasing and reading *Gameful Writing*! I hope you enjoyed reading this book.

My favorite teachers are books, and I will always be grateful to the many talented and inspiring people creating these beautiful wells of wisdom, inspiration, and encouragement. Among these amazing people are the award-winning authors and dear to my heart friends, Ariel and Shya Kane. Dear Ariel and Shya, thank you very much for all you do!

In the community that Ariel and Shya Kane created, I met my writing teacher Menna van Praag. She taught and inspired me on my journey of writing my very first book and also suggested to her students, one of whom I had a pleasure to be back in 2014, to treat writing our work-in-progress as a game. Dear Menna, thank you so much for your inspiration. That little game you suggested resulted in the fun that spread to all areas of my life and also into showing others the possibilities of living life gamefully.

Since I recall my writing journey here and those who helped me on the way, I need to mention and thank from all my heart, my niece Mihaela Breum and my dear friend Marcy, Marcella Belson. They read the manuscripts of my first two books and provided both honest and encouraging feedback.

Big thanks to Edin Hajder from Plus Consult, who introduced me to LeAnne Kline Christiansen, the CEO, Founder & Creator of the South Gate School (SGS) of Creative Writing in Aalborg. I have had the pleasure of teaching as a guest lecturer at SGS, for the past couple of years, especially on how to turn writing (and life) into fun games. LeAnne, thank you so much for this opportunity. Teaching writers is simply a gift and a huge honor!

LeAnne, thank you also so much for introducing me to the Black Label Writers' Club in Aalborg. Dear writer friends in the writers' club, I devoted this book to all of you and LeAnne, because of your tremendous support, encouragement, and cheering on my writing adventures. I get inspired at each of our monthly meetings, and I look forward to each one of them.

A big thank you to my dear friend Naz Ahsun for inviting me to appear on the first episode of "The Inspired Writer Podcast." Naz, thank you very much for your idea of rolling dice to figure out how many sentences to write next. This idea inspired not only what I call the introduction game (where I challenge my students to roll the dice and introduce themselves in as many sentences as they got on the dice), but it also gave me the idea for the two writing game variants with dice in this book.

A big thanks to my blog and newsletter subscribers as well as my followers on social media. Your feedback, opinions, and appreciation expressed in written form and sometimes in person mean the world to me.

I am hugely grateful to Alice Jago for editing this book. I was very much looking forward to reading this book after your edits because it's been quite some time since I have written a fiction book. It's the first one after so many non-fiction ones, and my first parable ever, and thus a unique experience. Thank you so much for editing so many of my books! They sound so much better. Including this one! I'm looking forward to our future projects together.

My biggest thanks go to my husband, Michael, and our children Niklas and Emma. This book, as with all the other projects I am passionate about, wouldn't exist without you. I love you!

About the Author

Victoria is a writer, coach, and consultant with a background in semiconductor physics, electronic engineering (with a Ph.D.), information technology, and business development. While being a non-gamer, Victoria came up with the term *Self-Gamification*, a gameful and playful self-help approach bringing anthropology, kaizen, and gamification-based methods together to increase the quality of life. She approaches all areas of her life this way. Due to the fun she has, while turning everything in her life into games, she intends never to stop designing and playing them.

Victoria is the author of the *5 Minute Perseverance Game*, *Self-Gamification Happiness Formula*, *The Who, What, When, Where, Why & How of Turning Life into Fun Games*, *Gameful Project Management*, *Gameful Healing*, *Gameful Isolation*, *Gameful Writing*, and *Gameful Mind*, as well as the instructor of the online course, *Motivate Yourself by Turning Your Life Into Fun Games*.

Gameful Writing is Book 4 and the first parable in the "Gameful Life" series. It is about approaching writing with excellence and ease in a gameful way — the Self-Gamification way.

Victoria was born and grew up in Moldova, lived in Germany for twelve years, and now lives in Aalborg, Denmark, with her husband and two children.

Visit or contact Victoria at

victoriaichizlibartels.com or optimistwriter.com.

Subscribe to Victoria's blog and news at

www.victoriaichizlibartels.com/subscribe-to-victorias-blog/.

By Victoria on Turning Life into Fun Games

Books
"Gameful Life" Series
Gameful Project Management:
Self-Gamification Based Awareness Booster for Your Project
Management Success
(Book 1)

Gameful Healing:
Almost a Memoir; Not Quite a Parable
(Book 2)

Gameful Isolation:
Making the Best of a Crisis, the Self-Gamification Way
(Book 3)

Gameful Writing:
Seven People, Seven Stories, Seven Lessons Learned
(Book 4)
(This book)

Gameful Mind
Solve the Puzzle of Your Enigmatic Subconscious
(Book 5)

193

Victoria Ichizli-Bartels

Standalone Books

The Who, What, When, Where, Why & How of Turning Life into Fun Games:
A Compressed Version of the Self-Gamification Happiness Formula

Self-Gamification Happiness Formula:
How to Turn Your Life into Fun Games

5 Minute Perseverance Game:
Play Daily for a Month and Become the Ultimate Procrastination Breaker

Online Course

Motivate Yourself by Turning Your Life Into Fun Games:
Practice Self-Gamification, a Unique Self-Help Approach Uniting Anthropology, Kaizen, and Gamification

Others by
Victoria Ichizli-Bartels

Other Motivational and Empowering Books
Cheerleading for Writers:
Discover How Truly Talented You Are

Turn Your No Into Yes:
15 Yes-Or-No Questions to Disentangle Your Project
Free e-book
(Available upon subscription to victoriaichizlibartels.com or optimistwriter.com)

Fiction Books
Between Grace and Abyss: A Short Story
(Also available as a free e-book upon subscription to victoriaichizlibartels.com or optimistwriter.com)

Nothing Is As It Seems: A Novelette

Seven Broken Pieces: A short story
(Prequel to series "A Life Upside Down")

A Spy's Daughter: A novella
(Book 1 in series "A Life Upside Down")

Victoria Ichizli-Bartels

The Truth About Family:
A novel inspired by true events

Business Books

Take Control of Your Business:
Learn what Business Rules are, discover that you are already using
them, then update them to maximize your business success

S1000D Books

brDoc, BREX, and Co.: S1000D Business Rules Made Easier

S1000D® Issue 4.1 and Issue 4.2 Navigation Map:
552+87 and 427+90 Business Rule Decision Points Arranged into
two Linear Topic Maps to Facilitate Learning, Understanding, and
Implementation of S1000D®

S1000D Issue 4.1 Untangled:
552+ Business Rules Decision Points Arranged into a Linear Topic
Map to Facilitate Learning, Understanding and Implementation of
S1000D
(unpublished, replaced by *S1000D® Issue 4.1 and Issue 4.2*
Navigation Map, see above)

Data Sheets and Templates

S1000D® Navigation Maps
https://www.victoriaichizlibartels.com/s1000d-navigation-
maps/

Printed in Great Britain
by Amazon

20413937R00113